INTERWEAVE PRESENTS

Classic Knit
SHAWLS

20 Timeless Designs
featuring Lace, Cables, & More

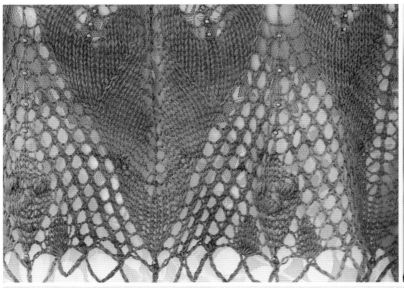

contents

introduction

If you Google "shawl," the first few results are the usual mainstream ones—Wikipedia, Etsy, some clothing e-commerce sites. But then, Ravelry knitted shawl pattern listings quickly take over the page. I think it's easy to say, knitters own the shawl in the Western world in this day and age.

Historically, shawls were functional layering garments, worn for warmth and in many cultures, modesty. But what's with modern knitters making all these lacey triangles and crescents and inventive asymmetrical shapes with short-rows and stripes and spurts of handpainted color? Something tells me this knitting craze has less to do with function or modesty and more to do with creative expression.

As an editor with Interweave, I watched the mid-2000s scarf trend ascend. We didn't have Ravelry then, but you couldn't miss the trend in publishing, in yarn shops, on the show floor of events such as Stitches. And then something else started to show up with more and more frequency . . . shawls. As scarf knitters advanced, and as they discovered lace, the traditional triangle flourished again. Evelyn Clark's gorgeous lace numbers in books such as *Scarf Style* and on the pages of *Interweave Knits* became hugely popular for us, and I walked many a knitter through their first shaped lace project on the phone, working on those projects. And then, in 2007, Ravelry showed up.

The collision of hand-dyed indie yarns, designers self-publishing, and knitters sharing their projects online made for a Shawl Explosion. We started printing more and more shawl patterns in Interweave magazines, as they garnered more likes and projects than other types of designs. We've published several books that emphasize shawls, including my *Free-Spirit Shawls* (Interweave, 2013), some patterns from which are included in this very collection. We sell more shawl project kits than any other kind of kit.

To this day, knitters love shawls. I don't think it's a trend anymore; it's a permanent archetype in our pantheon. There's no sizing; shawls use limited yarn, and they allow for such glorious explorations in color, pattern, and technique. Just look at the patterns in this book—such a variety in size, profile, complexity, and graphic impact. What a fun workbook for a creative life filled with yarn and charts and—please—lifelines.

I'm thrilled to present this collection of Interweave favorites; a good number of which are designs I curated for our knitting magazines and books over the years. And thank you to all the designers everywhere who puzzle out these patterns with their clever repeats and edgings and intricate charts. You keep us all obsessed.

Lisa Shroyer
Author, editor, and Content Strategist of Yarn + Fiber, Interweave

shawl Techniques

This book contains a variety of shawls from a variety of designers. As you'll see, there are many different ways to make, shape, and finish a shawl. Some of the more common methods of construction are covered in the following pages.

Triangles

While the top-down is probably the most popular triangle construction method, there are other ways to knit triangles. The bottom-up begins with a small cast-on and ends with a long bind-off edge (see diagram below). A wingspan-down triangle starts with a long cast-on that spans the width of the top edge and decreases at each edge down to the bottom point. And finally, a triangle can be worked side-to-side, with shaping at one edge to create the widening, then narrowing silhouette. We'll talk more about side to side shawls in the following section.

The Ennid Laceweight shawl (page 16) is contructed from side to side.

SIDE TO SIDE

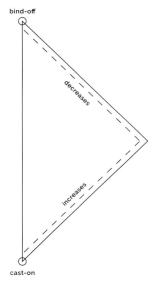

BOTTOM UP

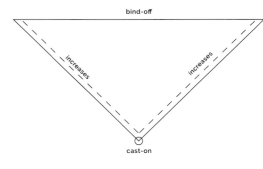

WINGSPAN DOWN

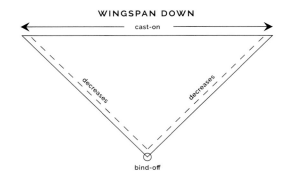

SEMICIRCLES

The Trillium shawl is worked from the top down and makes use of repeating increases worked within the lace pattern to achieve is semicircular shape. The semicircular shape of the Orangery shawl plays off the construction of a circular pi shawl.

CRESCENTS

Crescent shapes have a lot of flexibility. They can be short and deep with a strong upward curve or long and narrow with a slight upward curve. Lindsay is long and narrow, with a bottom-up short-row construction. The finished shape has a slight curvilinear profile.

Ship That Shawl is a small crescent with a more pronounced roundness. The garter-stitch body is worked top down, from the center out. Perpendicular panels are used to create visual interest.

SEMICIRCLE

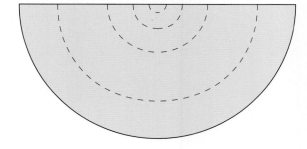

Orangery, above top (page 46), Trillium (page 100), Ship that Shawl, above bottm (page 34), Lindsay (page 104), and Galax (page 54) are all examples of semicircular and crescent shawls.

WORKING SIDE TO SIDE

Shawls with rounded silhouettes can be worked from side to side. This approach usually requires casting on a few stitches, then increasing evenly to the full depth, then decreasing back to the other end. The shaping can be worked solely at the outer edge or across the width of each row. Conversely, you can cast on the full number of stitches and create the shape with short-rows (see Short-Rows, below).

As previously mentioned, you can also work triangles side-to-side. By adjusting the rate of shaping, a sideways triangle can be short and deep or long and narrow. The Return Journey only increases (and then decreases) every fourth row, creating a long and shallow shape. The shaping is worked at the right-hand edge, allowing new repeats of the stitch pattern to be added every few inches. Madeleine features a more familiar triangular shape, with a deep center point. The increases (and then decreases) are worked every other row, so the shaping occurs twice as fast as in The Return Journey. In Rhoeas, by working side to side, the knitter can create a fringed edge as the shawl is knitted. See page 112 for more about this technique and how it suits sideways triangles.

short-rows

Many projects in this book use short-rows, but they achieve quite different results in each design. At the most basic, a short-row creates added depth in an isolated section of knitting. If you have 15 stitches and work a short-row across only 7 stitches, those 7 stitches will have 2 more rows worked than the surrounding stitches (the right-side row, then returning wrong-side row). You can see how short-rows add up to make curved shapes, with the center fabric deeper than the ends, which is ideal for crescent shawls. See Techniques for instructions on how to work in short-rows.

Note: Not all short-rows require wrapping the turning stitch. In garter stitch and other stitch patterns, the gap at the turn won't show. You can simply turn and continue working. Individual patterns will explain how to work their short-rows.

cast-ons and bind-offs for shawls

Most patterns in this book will recommend specific techniques for casting on and binding off. If the shawl you're working on doesn't recommend a specific technique, here are a few basic things to keep in mind when you knit shawls:

1 The edges should be elastic, so avoid working too tightly when you cast on and bind off. When it's blocked, your shawl will likely stretch and grow quite a bit. The edges will need to stretch and grow with the overall fabric.

2 You should become familiar with provisional cast-ons, especially when you work top-down triangles. See the Glossary for instructions.

When you bind off a large number of stitches, consider using two circular needles. You'll be able to spread the knitting out and methodically work a loose bind-off with consistent tension.

lace techniques

For lace projects, in addition to working loosely when casting on and binding off, you can also choose specific techniques that are looser than the standard (long-tail) cast-on and bind-off. See the Glossary at the back of the book for more information on these methods.

Cast-ons: Backward-loop cast-on, knitted cast-on.

Bind-off: Decrease bind-off.

make it pretty

WEAVING IN ENDS

Even if there is a definite right and wrong side to your shawl, a shawl is functionally a reversible project. Because people will see the wrong side, you should endeavor to weave in ends neatly. Consider these tips:

1 Join new balls a couple of inches in from the outer edge. This way, there won't be a knot or loose end right at the edge of the project.

2 Leave long tails and weave in the end for an inch more than you would in a normal project. See 4, below, for why.

3 Use duplicate stitch to weave in ends on the wrong side. If the project is worked in stockinette, then work reverse stockinette duplicate on the wrong side, tucked into the plainer areas of knitting (not through lace, for instance). If the project is worked in a combination of stitches, limit the weaving in to a consistent area and mimic that stitch in duplicate. If the project is worked in garter stitch, use garter-stitch duplicate (See the Glossary section on page 119 for more information on how to work these forms of duplicate stitch).

4 Weave in ends before blocking, but wait to trim the tails until after blocking. Stretching the fabric out will cause the tails to recede into the fabric, affecting the length of the end to be trimmed.

BLOCKING

Blocking is probably the most important step in shawl knitting. To achieve clean edges and ideal stretch across the fabric, use blocking wires or cotton string threaded evenly through the edges and stretched taut to create a kind of blocking wire. You will need T-pins to hold the wires in place. Your project may also require T-pins to shape out a scalloped edge. However, don't use T-pins to create the straight edges; they will create unintentional scalloping.

Try using Wool Wash to wet-block your shawl,

especially if it predominantly features lace. You want to really stretch lace fabric to its fullest extent to flatten the stitches and open the pattern. Soaking lace will help with this stretching. Heavier knits, such as worsted-weight shawls, don't require this kind of aggressive blocking. For The Return Journey, pinning the shawl flat, misting it with clean water, and then ironing the three points (over a damp towel) will do the trick. Always read your yarn label before blocking. If it contains synthetic content, ironing may not be a good idea. Superwash wools tend to lose body when wetted, but this may not matter with a shawl. Remember, to get an accurate gauge from your initial swatch, you should block and treat the swatch the same way you will treat the finished shawl.

continued shawl care

After you block your finished shawl, you may want to periodically reblock it. With wear and use, the shape may start to shrink back to its original dimensions. Lace may close up; you may find that the fabric wrinkles when left wadded in the backseat of your car. Washing and blocking will bring the life back to the knitting. And doing so may just reignite your passion for shawls all over again—taking you down the road to your next favorite project.

patterns

Each shawl in this book has been chosen for a reason whether that be unique construction, beautiful colorwork, lace details, or something else. As you flip through the patterns, don't be afraid to settle on a shawl that challenges you to move outside your comfort zone. You won't be disappointed.

Ennid Laceweight

SHAWL

DESIGNED BY Lucinda Guy

Simple, lace-light, and practical, the Ennid Shawl is reminiscent of the traditional garter-stitch triangular shawls once worn by Icelandic women on a daily basis. The small knitted edging lends an extra textural detail, which, once the shawl has been handwashed, softens and shapes up nicely.

finished size
About 82" (208.5 cm) wide across top edge and 23½" (59.5 cm) long from center of top edge to tip of lower point.

yarn
Laceweight (#0 Lace).

SHOWN HERE: Loðband Einband (100% Icelandic wool; 246 yd [225 ml/50 g): #9720 green, 5 balls.

needles
Size U.S. 3 (3.25 mm): 32" or 40" (80 or 100 cm) circular (cir).

Adjust needle size if necessary to obtain the correct gauge.

notions
Tapestry needle.

gauge
26 stitches and 44 rows = 4" (10 cm) in garter stitch.

NOTES

✤ The shawl is worked from side to side as a wide, shallow triangle. It begins at one top point, increases gradually along one selvedge to the center, then decreases to the other top point. The unshaped selvedge forms the straight top edge.

✤ For a larger or smaller shawl, repeat Rows 7–12 more or fewer times for the first half of the shawl, then repeat Rows 1–6 for the second half until 2 stitches remain. Every 12 rows (2 repeats) added or removed on each side of center will increase or decrease the overall width by about 2¼" (5.5 cm) and the length from the top edge to lower point by about ¾" (2 cm).

shawl

CO 2 sts. Inc for first half of shawl as foll:

Rows 1 (RS) and 2 (WS): Knit.

Row 3: K1f&b, k1—3 sts.

Rows 4 and 5: Knit.

Row 6: K1, k1f&b, k1—4 sts.

Rows 7 and 8: Knit.

Row 9: K1f&b, knit to end—1 st inc'd.

Rows 10 and 11: Knit.

Row 12: Knit to last 2 sts, k1f&b, k1—1 st inc'd.

Rep Rows 7–12 for patt 73 more times, or as desired (see Notes)—152 sts. Knit 2 rows—piece measures about 41" (104 cm) from CO. Dec for second half of shawl as foll:

Row 1: K1, k2tog, knit to end—1 st dec'd.

Rows 2 and 3: Knit.

Row 4: Knit to last 3 sts, k2tog, k1—1 st dec'd.

Rows 5 and 6: Knit.

Rep Rows 1–6 for patt 74 more times—2 sts rem. Knit 2 rows—piece measures about 82" (208.5 cm) from CO. BO all sts.

EDGING

Hold shawl with RS facing and straight top edge running across the bottom of the "pyramid" and join yarn to corner at right-hand side. With cir needle, pick up and knit 339 sts along shaped selvedge to center point (3 sts for every 4 rows), then 339 sts along other shaped edge to corner at left-hand side—678 sts total.

Row 1: (WS) *Insert tip of right needle into st on left needle as if to knit, wrap the yarn completely around tip of both needles once, then wrap the yarn around the right needle as if to knit and draw through a loop, then slip the old st and the wrap from the left needle; rep from * to end.

Note: This method of making elongated stitches is slightly different from wrapping the yarn twice around the needle for each stitch. This elongated stitch is formed in a single step, without having to drop any extra wraps on the following row, and will appear twisted at its base.

Row 2: (RS) Working all sts in the usual manner, BO 1 st, *work [k1, p1] 2 times in next st, turn work, BO 4 sts, turn work, slip first st on left needle to right needle, BO 2 sts; rep from * to end, fasten off last st.

finishing

Weave in loose ends. Carefully handwash shawl according to yarn-label instructions, roll in a towel to remove moisture, block to correct size, and allow to dry.

Junius Shaped
SHAWL

DESIGNED BY Corrina Ferguson

Lay Junius out flat and it might look like a typical large lace shawl. But drape it over your shoulders and you realize what a great layering piece it is. The clever increases create shoulder lines that allow the shawl to stay on even without a pin or other closure.

finished size

About 60" (152.5 cm) wide across top edge and 36" (91.5 cm) long from center of top edge to tip of lower point, after blocking.

yarn

Sportweight (#2 Fine).

SHOWN HERE: Dream In Color Perfectly Posh Sport (70% merino wool, 10% cashmere, 10% silk, 10% baby fine mohair; 320 yd [293 m]/3½ oz [100 g]): amberglass (gold), 3 skeins.

needles

Size U.S. 8 (5 mm): 40" (100 cm) circular (cir).

Adjust needle size if necessary to obtain the correct gauge.

notions

Markers (m); tapestry needle.

gauge

15 sts and 20 rows = 4" (10 cm) in Chart A after blocking.

set-up

CO 70 sts. Work the Set-up Charts as foll: Work Right-Side Set-up Chart, then Center and Left-Side Set-up Chart. Cont to work charts in this way through Row 10, placing markers as indicated on Row 10—98 sts.

body

Work the Body Chart as foll: Work to marker, [work Chart A once, Chart B once] twice, work Chart A once, work to end of Body Chart. Cont to work charts in this way through Row 40—178 sts.

RIGHT-SIDE SET-UP CHART

CENTER AND LEFT-SIDE SET-UP CHART

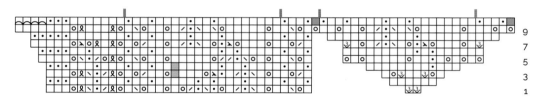

	k on RS; p on WS
•	p on RS; k on WS
☀	sl 1 wyf
▧	knit st to begin next Chart B
▨	no stitch
ℓ	k1tbl
o	yo
∕	k2tog on RS, p2tog on WS
↘	ssk
⅄	k3tog
⅄	sl 1, k2tog, psso
↘	ssk on RS over 1 st from edging and 1 st from body
↓	k1, yo, k1 in same st
↓	k1, yo, k1, yo, k1 in same st
⌒	bind off 1 st
☐	pattern repeat
▮	marker position

CHART A

CHART B

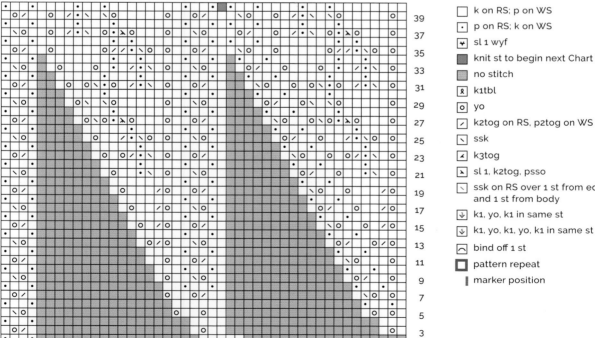

	k on RS; p on WS
•	p on RS; k on WS
↙	sl 1 wyf
▨	knit st to begin next Chart B
▨	no stitch
℞	k1tbl
o	yo
/	k2tog on RS, p2tog on WS
\	ssk
⅄	k3tog
⅄	sl 1, k2tog, psso
⌐	ssk on RS over 1 st from edging and 1 st from body
⅄	k1, yo, k1 in same st
⅄	k1, yo, k1, yo, k1 in same st
⌢	bind off 1 st
◻	pattern repeat
ǀ	marker position

BODY CHART

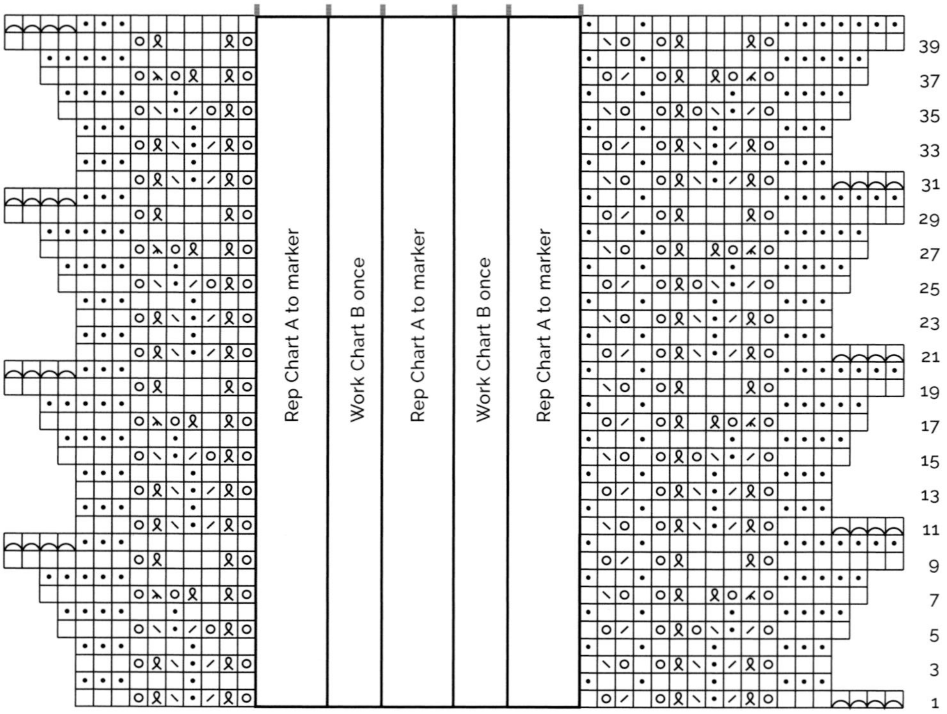

Legend:
- □ k on RS; p on WS
- · p on RS; k on WS
- ⤓ sl 1 wyf
- ▨ knit st to begin next Chart B
- ▨ no stitch
- ℓ k1tbl
- ○ yo
- ╱ k2tog on RS, p2tog on WS
- ╲ ssk
- ◿ k3tog
- ◺ sl 1, k2tog, psso
- □ ssk on RS over 1 st from edging and 1 st from body
- ⤓ k1, yo, k1 in same st
- ⤓ k1, yo, k1, yo, k1 in same st
- ⌢ bind off 1 st
- □ pattern repeat
- | marker position

EDGING CHART

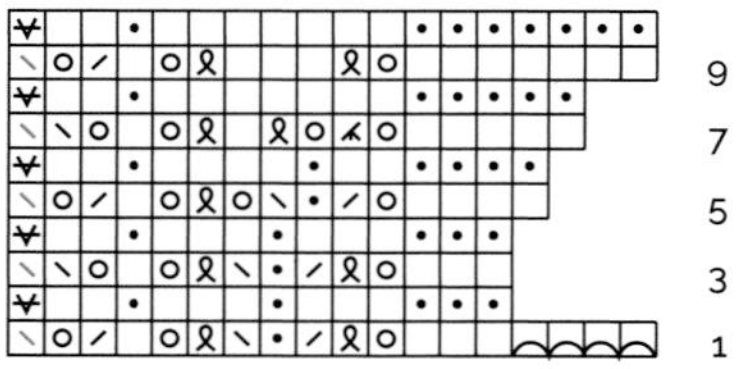

Work the Body Chart as foll:
Work to marker, work Chart A twice, work Chart B once, work Chart A 3 times, work Chart B once, work Chart A twice, work to end of Body Chart. Cont to work charts in this way through Row 40—258 sts.

Work the Body Chart as foll:
Work to marker, work Chart A 3 times, work Chart B once, work Chart A 5 times, work Chart B once, work Chart A 3 times, work to end of Body Chart. Cont to work charts in this way through Row 20—306 sts.

EDGING

Work Edging Chart over first 18 sts, joining edging sts to body sts on needle with an ssk at the end of every RS row. Rep Rows 1–10 of Edging Chart until 14 sts rem from opposite edge, end with Row 4 of chart—14 sts. Graft last row to rem 14 sts.

finishing

Sew cast-on edge together. Weave in all ends, but do not trim. Block using pins or wires to bring out points and block the shawl into a rounded rectangle shape. Trim ends.

Junius Shaped shawl

Ilme's Autumn
TRIANGLE

DESIGNED BY **Nancy Bush**

An expert on Estonian knitting, Nancy Bush modeled this shawl after the small triangular scarves currently made along the west coast in the vicinity of Haapsalu. Worked from the point up to the top edge, this shawl incorporates classic patterns, such as a scalloped outer edge, a wide openwork border, and a smaller openwork pattern in the center.

finished size

About 54" (137 cm) wide across top edge and 36" (91.5 cm) long from center of top edge to bottom point, after blocking.

yarn

Laceweight (#0 Lace).

SHOWN HERE: Elemental Affects Shetland Rustic Lace (100% North American Shetland wool; 660 yd [600 m]/100 g): #016 bronze, 2 skeins.

needles

Size U.S. 4 (3.5 mm): 32" (80 cm) or longer circular (cir) and 2 double-pointed (dpn) for Kitchener st or three-needle bind-off.

Adjust needle size if necessary to obtain the correct gauge.

notions

Markers (m); tapestry needle; coil-less safety pin or removable marker; blocking wires and T-pins.

gauge

20 sts and 32 rows = 4" (10 cm) in St st, before blocking.

17 sts and 28 rows = 4" (10 cm) in allover lace patt from Top charts, after blocking.

Slipped Selvedge Sts
On both RS and WS, slip the first st as if to purl with yarn in front (pwise wyf), then bring the yarn to the back of the work between the needles.

5-st Nupp
With RS facing, very loosely work [k1, yo, k1, yo, k1] all in same st—5 sts made from 1 st. On the foll WS row, purl these 5 sts tog to dec them back to 1 st.

Gathered Sts
(worked over 3 sts)
K3tog but do not slip sts from needle, yo, then knit the same 3 sts tog again, then sl all 3 sts from needle tog—3 sts made from 3 sts.

shawl

With two strands of yarn held tog, use the knitted method (see Glossary) to CO 351 sts. Drop one strand and continue with a single strand of yarn throughout.

Knit 2 rows, ending with a WS row.

LOWER EDGE PATTERN

Establish patts from Row 1 of both Right Lower Edge and Left Lower Edge charts as foll: (RS) Work first 4 sts of Right Lower Edge chart, place marker (pm), work next 19 sts and dec them to 18 sts as shown, work 16-st patt rep 8 times, work next 24 sts of chart, k1 for last st of chart (center st) and place a coil-less safety pin or removable marker in center st; work the first 25 sts of Left Lower Edge chart, work the 16-st patt rep 8 times, work next 18 sts of chart and dec them to 17 sts as shown, pm, work last 4 sts of chart—349 sts rem; 1 marked center st; 170 patt sts and 4 border sts at each side.

Note: Move the marker in the center st up as the work progresses so you can easily identify the center st.

Work Rows 2–25 of charts, ending with a RS row—313 sts rem; 1 marked center st; 148 patt sts and 8 border sts at each side.

FIRST GATHERED STITCHES PATTERN

Rows 1 and 3: (WS) Sl 1 pwise wyf, k7, slip marker (sl m), knit to last 8 sts, sl m, k8.

Rows 2 and 4: (RS) Sl 1 pwise wyf, k7, sl m, [sl 1, k1, psso], knit to 1 st before center st, [sl 1, k2tog, psso], knit to 2 sts before next m, k2tog, sl m, k8—4 sts dec'd each row; 305 sts after Row 4; 1 marked center st; 144 patt sts and 8 border sts at each side.

Row 5: Sl 1 pwise wyf, k7, sl m, purl to last 8 sts, sl m, k8.

Row 6: (RS; gathered sts row) Sl 1 pwise wyf, k7, sl m, sl 1, k1, psso, [work gathered sts (see Stitch Guide) over 3 sts] 47 times to 1 st before center st, sl 1, k2tog, psso, [work gathered st over 3 sts] 47 times, k2tog, sl m, k8—4 sts dec'd.

Row 7: Rep Row 5.

Rows 8 and 10: Rep Row 2—4 sts dec'd each row.

chart, work the 16-st patt rep 6 times, work next 23 sts of chart dec them to 22 sts as shown, sl m, work last 8 sts of chart—285 sts rem; 1 marked center st; 134 patt sts and 8 border sts at each side.

Work Rows 2–27 of charts, ending with a RS row—233 sts rem; 1 marked center st; 108 patt sts and 8 border sts at each side.

SECOND GATHERED STITCHES PATTERN

Rows 1 and 3: (WS) Sl 1 pwise wyf, k7, slip marker (sl m), knit to last 8 sts, sl m, k8.

Rows 2 and 4: (RS) Sl 1 pwise wyf, k7, sl m, sl 1, k1, psso, knit to 1 st before center st, sl 1, k2tog, psso, knit to 2 sts before next m, k2tog, sl m, k8—4 sts dec'd each row; 225 sts after Row 4; 1 marked center st; 104 patt sts and 8 border sts at each side.

Row 5: Sl 1 pwise wyf, k7, sl m, purl to last 8 sts, sl m, k8.

Row 6: (RS; gathered sts row) Sl 1 pwise wyf, k7, sl m, sl 1, k1, psso, [work gathered sts over 3 sts] 33 times to 3 sts before center st, k2, sl 1, k2tog, psso, k2, [work gathered st over 3 sts] 33 times, k2tog, sl m, k8—4 sts dec'd.

Row 7: Rep Row 5.

Rows 8 and 10: Rep Row 2—4 sts dec'd each row.

Rows 9 and 11: Rep Row 1.

Row 12: Rep Row 2—4 sts dec'd; 209 sts rem; 1 marked center st; 96 patt sts and 8 border sts at each side.

Row 13: Rep Row 5.

TOP PATTERN

Establish patts from Row 1 of both Right Top and Left Top charts as foll: (RS) Work first 8 sts of Right Top chart, sl m, work next 21 sts of chart and dec them to 20 sts as shown, work 6-st patt rep 9 times, work next 20 sts of chart to 1 st before marked center st, sl 1, k2tog, psso; work the first 21 sts of Left Top chart, work the 6-st patt rep 9 times, work next 20 sts of chart and dec them to 19 sts as shown, sl m, work last 8 sts of chart—205 sts rem; 1 marked center st; 94 patt sts and 8 border sts at each side.

Rows 9 and 11: Rep Row 1.

Row 12: Rep Row 2—4 sts dec'd; 289 sts rem; 1 marked center st; 136 patt sts and 8 border sts at each side.

Row 13: Rep Row 5.

DIAMOND BORDER PATTERN

Establish patts from Row 1 of both Right Diamond Border and Left Diamond Border charts (see pages 30 and 31) as foll: (RS) Work first 8 sts of Right Diamond Border chart, sl m, work next 24 sts of chart dec them to 23 sts as shown, work 16-st patt rep 6 times, work next 15 sts of chart to 1 st before marked center st, work [sl 1, k2tog, psso] in next 3 sts as shown; work the first 16 sts of Left Diamond Border

LOWER TOP

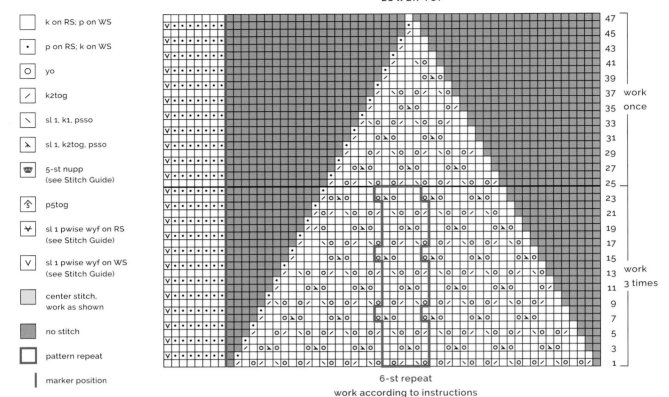

Legend:

□	k on RS; p on WS
•	p on RS; k on WS
O	yo
/	k2tog
\	sl 1, k1, psso
⋏	sl 1, k2tog, psso
♛	5-st nupp (see Stitch Guide)
⏫	p5tog
⤈	sl 1 pwise wyf on RS (see Stitch Guide)
V	sl 1 pwise wyf on WS (see Stitch Guide)
▨	center stitch, work as shown
▨	no stitch
▢	pattern repeat
│	marker position

Row numbers (right side, LOWER TOP): 47, 45, 43, 41, 39, 37, 35, 33, 31, 29, 27, 25, 23, 21, 19, 17, 15, 13, 11, 9, 7, 5, 3, 1

work once (rows 25–47)

work 3 times (rows 1–23)

6-st repeat
work according to instructions

LEFT DIAMOND BORDER

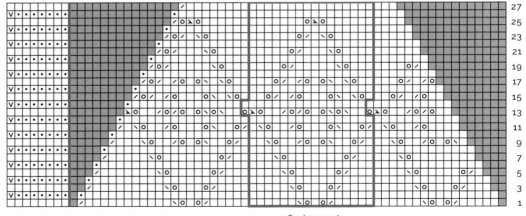

Row numbers (right side, LEFT DIAMOND BORDER): 27, 25, 23, 21, 19, 17, 15, 13, 11, 9, 7, 5, 3, 1

16-st repeat
work 6 times

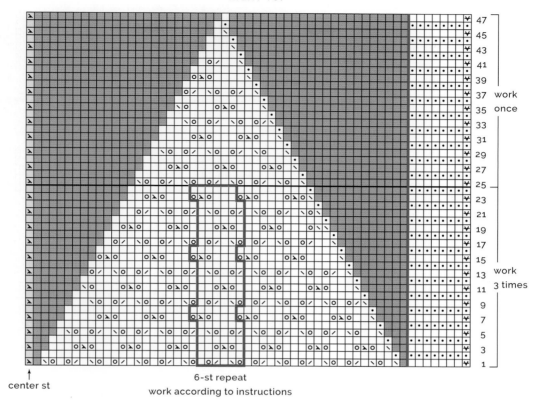

center st

6-st repeat
work according to instructions

work once

work 3 times

RIGHT DIAMOND BORDER

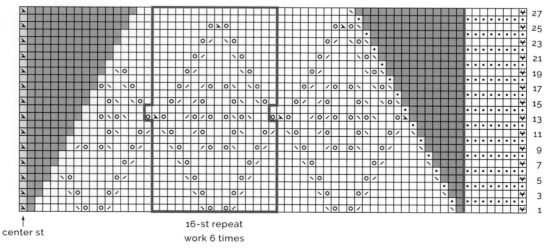

center st

16-st repeat
work 6 times

LOWER LEFT EDGE

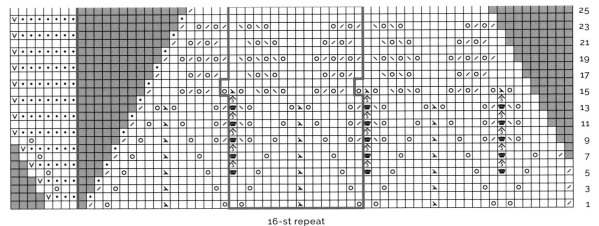

16-st repeat
work 8 times

RIGHT LOWER EDGE

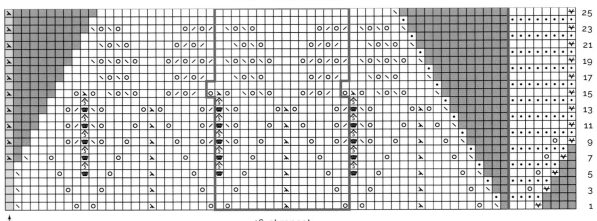

center st

16-st repeat
work 8 times

□ k on RS; p on WS	⋌ sl 1, k2tog, psso	▓ center stitch, work as shown
• p on RS; k on WS	⬚ 5-st nupp (see Stitch Guide)	▓ no stitch
○ yo	⬆ p5tog	☐ pattern repeat
╱ k2tog	↯ sl 1 pwise wyf on RS (see Stitch Guide)	▏ marker position
╲ sl 1, k1, psso	V sl 1 pwise wyf on WS (see Stitch Guide)	

Work Rows 2–24 of chart—161 sts rem; 1 marked center st; 72 patt sts and 8 border sts at each side.

Work Rows 1–24 of chart once more, working each 6-st patt rep 5 times—113 sts rem; 1 marked center st; 48 patt sts and 8 border sts at each side.

Work Rows 1–24 of chart once more, working each 6-st patt rep once—65 sts rem; 1 marked center st; 24 patt sts and 8 border sts at each side.

Work Rows 25–47 of chart once—19 sts rem; 1 marked center st; 1 patt st and 8 border sts at each side.

Next row: (WS) Removing markers as you come to them, sl 1 pwise wyf, k6, sl 1 kwise, k3tog, psso, k8—16 sts rem.

Cut yarn, leaving a 12" (30.5 cm) tail.

finishing

Arrange rem 16 sts on two dpns so that there are 8 sts on each needle. Hold needles parallel with WS of shawl facing tog and RS facing out. Thread yarn tail onto tapestry needle and use the Kitchener st (see Glossary) to graft the sts tog (for an alternate finish, work a three-needle bind-off to join the two sets of 8 sts).

Weave in loose ends.

Handwash gently in mild soap and warm water. Rinse and squeeze out excess moisture.

Place damp shawl on clean, flat surface and thread a blocking wire through each stitch along the straight top edge and through each [sl 1, k2tog, psso] point along the lower edges. Stretch the shawl to measurements, using T-pins to pin the wires in place. Allow to air-dry thoroughly before removing pins.

Ship That
SHAWL

DESIGNED BY **Meg Burcl**

The gradual color transitions of an ombré-dyed yarn take center stage in this top-down shawl. A coordinating solid yarn worked in a perpendicular panel adds visual interest, while short rows work to create a distinctive shoulder-hugging shape.

finished size
Size 48" (122 cm) wide and 10½" (26.5 cm) tall

yarn
Fingering weight (#1 Super Fine)

SHOWN HERE: Yarn Freia Fine Handpaint Yarns Fingering Ombré (75% wool, 25% nylon; 322 yd [294 ml]/ 75 g): oro azteca (MC), 1 skein.

Freia Fine Handpaint Yarns Fingering (75% wool, 25% nylon; 215 yd [197 ml]/50 g): elephant (CC), 1 skein.

needles
Size 5 (3.75 mm): 32" (80 cm) circular (cir) needle.

Adjust needle size if necessary to obtain the correct gauge.

notions
Markers (m); removable m; stitch holders for 3–4 sts; tapestry needle.

gauge
23 sts and 49 rows = 4" (10 cm) in garter st.

garter tab

With MC, CO 3 sts. Knit 6 rows.

Next row: (RS) K3, working along selvedge edge, pick up and knit 3 sts (1 st in each garter ridge), then pick up and knit 1 st in each CO st—9 sts total.

Set-up row: (WS) K4, place marker (pm), k1, pm, k4.

section I

Row 1: (RS) With MC, k3, M1R, knit to m, sl m, M1R, knit to m, M1L, sl m, knit to last 3 sts, M1L, k3—4 sts inc'd.

Row 2: K3, M1R, knit to last 3 sts, M1L, k3—2 sts inc'd.

Rep last 2 rows 18 more times—123 sts: 42 sts at each end, 39 sts between m. With CC, rep Rows 1 and 2 once—129 sts: 44 sts at each end, 41 sts between m. With MC, rep Rows 1 and 2 ten times—189 sts: 64 sts at each end, 61 sts between m.

section 2

Next row: (RS) With CC, place 3 sts on holder, knit to last 3 sts, sl 3 pwise wyb—186 sts. Slide sts to other end of needle. With CC and RS facing, with live sts on left needle, CO 11 sts onto left needle—197 sts.

Row 1: (RS) K10, ssk, turn.

Row 2: K11.

Rep last 2 rows 60 more times, removing m on last RS row. Turn corner using short-rows as foll:

Short-row 1: (RS) K2, mark yarn (see Notes), turn.

Short-row 2: (WS) K2.

Short-row 3: K2, k2tog (marked yarn with next st), k1, mark yarn, turn.

Short-row 4: K4.

Short-row 5: K4, k2tog (marked yarn with next st), k1, mark yarn, turn.

Short-row 6: K6.

Short-row 7: K6, k2tog (marked yarn with next st), k1, mark yarn, turn.

Short-row 8 K8.

NOTES

✦ This shawl is worked in garter stitch from the center neck down and outward, with the exception of the solid-colored panel, which is worked perpendicularly.

✦ The sample was made using the Japanese short-row technique, although you may use whatever technique works best for you. With this method, when ending a short-row, clip a removable marker around the working yarn to mark the yarn at the turning point before beginning the wrong-side row, then work the first wrong-side stitch as usual. When working across the short-rows, use the marker to lift the yarn and place this strand onto the left needle, then remove the marker. Work the strand with the next stitch as a k2tog. For a free video on *4 Ways to Wrap Short-Rows*, visit bit.ly/ShortRowVideo.

Short-row 9: K8, k2tog (marked yarn with next st), k1, mark yarn, turn.

Short-row 10: K10.

Short-row 11: K10, place marked yarn onto right needle, ssk, pass marked yarn over, turn.

Short-row 12: K11.

Next row: (RS) K10, ssk, turn. Next row K11. Rep last 2 rows 59 more times, removing m on last RS row. Turn corner using short-rows as foll:

Short-row 1: (RS) K10, mark yarn, turn.

Short-row 2: (WS) K10.

Short-row 3: K8, mark yarn, turn.

Short-row 4: K8.

Short-row 5: K6, mark yarn, turn.

Short-row 6: K6.

Short-row 7: K4, mark yarn, turn.

Short-row 8: K4.

Short-row 9: K2, mark yarn, turn.

Short-row 10: K2.

Next row: (RS) K2, [k2tog (marked yarn with next st), k1] 4 times, place marked yarn onto right needle, ssk, pass marked yarn over, turn. Next row K11. Next row K10, ssk, turn. Next row K11. Rep last 2 rows 58 more times—15 sts rem. Dec row (RS) K10, ssk, k3—14 sts rem. Next row Knit. Dec row Knit to last 4 sts, k2tog, k2—1 st dec'd. Next row Knit. Rep last 2 rows 9 more times—4 sts rem. Place sts on holder.

Row 1: With CC and RS facing, k3 from holder (at beg of RS row), pick up and knit 10 sts from CO edge of section 2—13 sts.

Row 2: Knit.

Row 3: K2, ssk, knit to end—1 st dec'd.

Row 4: Knit.

Rep last 2 rows 8 more times—4 sts rem. Leave sts on needle.

section 3

Row 1: (RS) With MC, k4, pick up and knit 213 sts (1 st in each garter ridge of section 2), k4 from holder—221 sts.

Row 2: K74, pm, k73, pm, k74.

Row 3: K3, M1R, knit to m, sl m, M1R, knit to m, M1L, sl m, knit to last 3 sts, M1L, k3—4 sts inc'd.

Row 4: K3, M1R, knit to last 3 sts, M1L, k3—2 sts inc'd.

Rep last 2 rows 8 more times—275 sts: 92 sts at each end, 91 sts between m. With CC, rep Rows 3 and 4 once. With MC, rep Rows 3 and 4 once. Rep last 4 rows 4 more times—335 sts: 112 sts at each end, 111 sts between m. With MC, rep Rows 3 and 4 three times, then work Row 3 once more—357 sts: 119 sts at each end, 119 sts between m. With WS facing, BO all sts kwise.

finishing

Weave in ends. Block, keeping top edge straight.

Diospyros
SHAWL

DESIGNED BY **Andrea Jurgrau**

Inspired by leaf motifs seen in vintage art lace tablecloths, Andrea Jurgrau designed this shawl with delicate retro flare. Estonian bobbles, or nupps, add texture to the leaf motifs, and bronze beads applied with a crochet hook highlight the stems of larger leaves. Knit in a lush silk-cashmere blend, it adds a little bit of luxury to any look.

finished size

About 70" (178 cm) wide and 17" (43 cm) long at center back, blocked; about 62" (157.5 cm) wide and 15" (38 cm) long at center back, after relaxing.

yarn

Laceweight (#0 Lace).

SHOWN HERE:
Jade Sapphire Silk/Cashmere 2-ply (55% silk, 45% Mongolian cashmere; 400 yd [366 m]/55 g): #148 Elysian Fields, 2 skeins.

needles

U.S. size 4 (3.5 mm): 40" (100 cm) circular (cir).

Adjust needle size if necessary to obtain the correct gauge.

notions

About 20 g of 8/0 Miyuki Japanese seed beads (shown in #457 metallic dark bronze); size 14 (0.75 mm) steel crochet hook (or size to fit beads); size 4 (2 mm) steel crochet hook for bind-off; tapestry needle; flexible blocking wires; T-pins;

6" (15 cm) stick pin (pin shown is MEI FA hair sticks from Shaunebazner.com).

gauge

9 sts and 16 rows = 2" (5 cm) in garter st, relaxed after blocking.

NOTES

+ A circular needle is used to accommodate the large number of sts. Do not join; work back and forth in rows.
+ Beads are added with a crochet hook (see page 43).

shawl

Using the cable method (see Glossary), CO 250 sts. Do not join. Work back and forth in rows.

Knit 2 rows—1 garter ridge.

Work short-rows as foll:

Short-row 1: With RS facing, knit to last 20 sts, turn work so WS is facing, sl 1 knitwise with yarn in back (kwise wyb) knit to last 20 sts, turn work.

Short-row 2: With RS facing, sl 1 kwise wyb, knit to last 40 sts, turn work so WS is facing, sl 1 kwise wyb, knit to last 40 sts, turn work.

Short-row 3: With RS facing, sl 1 kwise wyb, knit to last 60 sts, turn work so WS is facing, sl 1 kwise wyb, knit to last 60 sts, turn work.

Short-row 4: With RS facing, sl 1 kwise wyb, knit to last 80 sts, turn work so WS is facing, sl 1 kwise wyb, knit to last 80 sts, turn work.

applying beads with a crochet hook

This method allows precise placement of the bead in an individual stitch and is the method used for most of the projects in this book. Although it's easier to put the bead on the stitch before it is knitted, so doing can compromise the tension on that stitch.

Work to the stitch designated for bead placement, work the stitch as specified in the instructions, slip a bead onto the shaft of a crochet hook, remove the knitted stitch from the knitting needle, and lift the stitch just worked with the hook (Figure 1). Slide the bead onto the stitch just worked, return that stitch to the left needle, adjust the tension, then slip that stitch onto the right knitting needle (Figure 2).

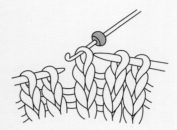

Figure 1

Figure 2

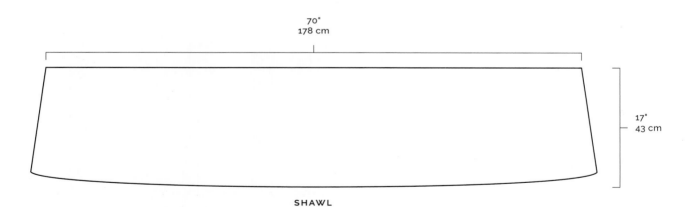

70"
178 cm

17"
43 cm

SHAWL

DIOSPYROS CHART

☐	knit on RS; purl on WS
•	purl on RS; knit on WS
ℛ	k1tbl on RS; p1tbl on WS
⤵	[k1, p1] in same stitch
╲	ssk
╱	k2tog
○	yo
■	place bead
⤋	[k1, yo, k1, yo, k1, yo, k1, yo, k1] in same stitch
⤓9	p9tog
⊥	pick up and knit 1 st from between the sts, 3 rows below
⋀	s2kp
🅜	s2kp, place bead
⬆3	gather 3
⬆4	gather 4
⬆7	gather 7
▩	no stitch
0	crochet chain
☐	pattern repeat

Short-row 5: With RS facing, sl 1 kwise wyb, knit to last 100 sts, turn work so WS is facing, sl 1 kwise wyb, knit to last 100 sts, turn work.

Short-row 6: With RS facing, sl 1 kwise wyb, knit to last 120 sts, turn work so WS is facing, sl 1 kwise wyb, knit to last 120 sts, turn work.

Next row: With RS facing, sl 1 kwise wyb, knit to end.

Next row: (WS) Knit.

Adding beads with smaller crochet hook (see page 43) as specified, work Rows 1–84 of Diospyros chart—437 sts.

With the larger crochet hook, use the gathered crochet method (see Glossary) to BO as foll: [gather 3, chain 8] 4 times, gather 7, chain 8, gather 3, chain 8, *gather 7, chain 8, [gather 4, chain 8] 2 times, gather 3, chain 8, [gather 4, chain 8] 2 times, gather 7, chain 8, gather 3, chain 8; rep from * 10 more times, gather 7, chain 8, [gather 3, chain 8] 3 times, gather 3.

Cut yarn, leaving a 9" (23 cm) tail. Pull tail through rem loop to secure.

finishing

Weave in loose ends but do not trim tails.

Soak in cool water for at least 30 minutes. Roll in a towel to remove excess water.

Weave flexible wires along top "straight" edge and both selvedges. Place on flat padded surface, stretch to finished measurements, and pin out each chain loop along the BO edge.

Allow to air-dry thoroughly before removing wires and pins.

Trim tails on woven-in ends.

Orangery
SHAWL

DESIGNED BY Carol Feller

The art deco Orangery Shawl shows off the simplicity of pi shawls, which have all the increases in single rounds. The design allows for relaxing knitting that lets the yarn colors shine. Combined with the welted garter edge that blends the complementary colors together, you have an undemanding knit that is perfect for gradient yarn or color progressions.

finished size

53" (135 cm) wide and 19" (48.5 cm) tall at center.

yarn

Fingering (#1 Super Fine)

SHOWN HERE: SweetGeorgia Yarns Tough Love Sock; (80% superwash merino, 20% nylon;

425 yd [388 m]/4 oz [115 g]): evergreen (blue/green; A), fern (dark green; B), and basil (light green; C), 1 skein each.

needles

Size 6 (4 mm): 40" (100 cm) circular (cir).

Adjust needle size if necessary to obtain the correct gauge.

notions

Removable markers (m); tapestry needle.

gauge

18 sts and 37 rows = 4" (10 cm) in garter st.

shawl

With A, CO 3 sts. Knit 6 rows, sl first st of every row (see Notes); do not turn after last row. Rotate work and pick up and knit 3 sts down selvedge (1 st in each sl st), then 3 sts along CO edge—9 sts.

Next row: (WS) Sl 1, k8. Inc row (RS) Sl 1, k2, [yo, k1f&b] 3 times, yo, k3—16 sts. Knit 5 rows.

Inc row: (RS) Sl 1, k2, [k1, yo] 10 times, k3—26 sts. Knit 1 WS row. Join B (see Notes) and knit 2 rows. With A, knit 6 rows.

Inc row: (RS) With B, sl 1, k2, [k1, yo] 20 times, k3—46 sts. Knit 15 rows. With A, knit 2 rows.

Inc row: (RS) With B, sl 1, k2, [k1, yo] 40 times, k3—86 sts. Knit 15 rows. With A, knit 2 rows. Break A.

With B, knit 14 rows. Join C.

Inc row: (RS) With C, sl 1, k2, [k1, yo] 80 times, k3—166 sts. Knit 19 rows. *With B, knit 2 rows. With C, knit 20 rows. Rep from * once more.

Inc row: (RS) With C, sl 1, k2, [k1, yo] 159 times, k4—325 sts. Knit 5 rows.

EDGING

With B, work Rows 1–6 of Edging chart. With C, work Rows 7–12 of chart. Rep last 12 rows once more. Break C. With B, work Rows 1–6 of chart. With A, work Rows 7–12 of chart. Rep last 12 rows 2 more times. With A, BO all sts as foll: k1, *k1, sl 2 sts to left needle, k2tog tbl; rep from * to end.

finishing

Weave in ends. Block to finished measurements.

NOTES

✦ This shawl is worked back and forth in rows from the top down. A circular needle is used to accommodate the large number of stitches.

✦ Slip the first stitch of every row purlwise with yarn in front.

✦ When a color is unused for only a few rows, carry it up the side of the work until it is needed again. Bring new color under old color at each color change.

EDGING

11-st repeat

	k on RS; p on WS
	p on RS; k on WS
	k2tog
	ssk
	sl 1 pwise wyb on RS; sl 1 pwise wyf on WS
	k1f&b
	pattern repeat

Grand Army Plaza
SHAWL

DESIGNED BY Melissa Wehrle

This shawl design was inspired by the tucked-away niches of green that you can find all over New York City. The garter-based lace motifs are mostly reversible, and the resulting fabric doesn't curl. So when it's draped over your shoulders, all your knitting will be seen and appreciated!

finished size
About 54" (137 cm) across top edge and 24" (61 cm) long from center of top edge to lower point, blocked.

yarn
Laceweight (#0 Lace).

SHOWN HERE: Sundara Yarn Silk Lace (100% silk; 1000 yd [914 m]/100 g): island breeze, 1 skein.

needles
Size U.S. 4 (3.5 mm): 24" (60 cm) cir needle and one double-pointed needle (dpn).

Adjust needle size, if necessary, to obtain the correct gauge; exact gauge is not critical for this project.

notions
Tapestry needle; rustproof blocking pins.

gauge
16 sts and 24 rows = 4" (10 cm) in average gauge of lace patts, after blocking.

STITCH GUIDE

Roman Stripe

(worked on an even number of patt sts + 4 edge sts)

Row 1: K2 (edge sts), *yo, k1; rep from * to last 2 sts, k2 (edge sts)—sts have inc'd to twice the original patt sts, plus 2 edge sts at each side.

Row 2: K2, purl to last 2 sts, k2.

Row 3: K2, *k2tog; rep from * to last 2 sts, k2—sts have dec'd to original number.

Rows 4 and 5: K2, *yo, k2tog; rep from to last 2 sts, k2.

Rows 6 and 7: Knit.

Rep Rows 1–7 for patt.

Madeira Mesh

(multiple of 6 sts + 7)

Rows 1–6: K2, *yo, p3tog, yo, k3; rep from *, to last 5 sts, yo, p3tog, yo, k2.

Rows 7–12: K2, *k3, yo, p3tog, yo; rep from * to last 5 sts, k5.

Rep Rows 1–12 for patt.

Double Fagoting

(multiple of 4 sts + 1)

Row 1: (RS) K3, *yo, p3tog, yo, k1; rep from * to last 2 sts, k2.

Row 2: (WS) K2, p2tog, yo, k1, *yo, p3tog, yo, k1; rep from * last 4 sts, yo, p2tog, k2.

Rep Rows 1 and 2 for patt.

NOTES

✛ The shawl begins in the center of the upper edge and is worked downward with increases to shape the half circle.

✛ The lace edging is worked perpendicularly to the body of the shawl, joining one edging stitch together with one live shawl stitch at the end of every even-numbered edging row until all the shawl stitches have been consumed.

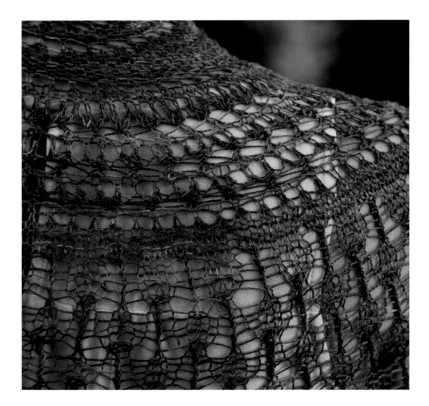

shawl

CO 8 sts.

Row 1: Knit.

Row 2: K2, *yo, k1; rep from * to last 2 sts, k2—12 sts.

Rows 3–5: Knit.

Row 6: K2, *yo, k1; rep from * to last 2 sts, k2—20 sts.

Rows 7–12: Knit.

Row 13: K2, *yo, k1; rep from * to last 2 sts, k2—36 sts.

Rows 14–25: Knit.

Row 26: K2, *yo, k1; rep from * to last 2 sts, k2—68 sts.

Rows 27–28: Knit.

Rows 29–49: Work Rows 1–7 of Roman Stripe patt (see Stitch Guide) 3 times.

Rows 50–51: Knit.

Row 52: K2, *yo, k1; rep from * to last 2 sts, k2—132 sts.

Rows 53–58: Knit.

Row 59: K2, M1 (see Glossary), knit to end—133 sts.

Rows 60–101: Work Rows 1–12 of Madeira Mesh patt (see Stitch Guide) 3 times, then work Rows 1–6 once more.

Row 102: K2, *yo, k1; rep from * to last 3 sts, k3—261 sts.

Rows 103–142: Work Rows 1 and 2 of Double Fagoting patt (see Stitch Guide) 20 times.

Rows 143–145: Knit.

LACE EDGING

Turn the work so the end of the cir needle with working yarn is in your right hand. Use the backward-loop method (see Glossary) to CO 10 sts onto the end of the right needle—271 sts total; 261 live shawl sts, 10 edging sts. Turn the work so the end of the cir needle with the new CO sts is in your left hand and use the dpn instead of the other cir needle tip to work the edging as foll:

Setup row: K9, k2tog (last edging st tog with shawl st after it), turn work—10 edging sts; 1 shawl st joined.

Row 1: K2, yo, k2tog, k2, k2tog, yo, k2.

Row 2: K3, yo, k2, yo, k4, k2tog (last edging st tog with next shawl st), turn work—12 edging sts; 1 shawl st joined.

Row 3: K2, yo, k10—13 edging sts.

Row 4: BO 3 sts (1 st rem on right needle after last BO), k8, k2tog (last edging st tog with next shawl st), turn work—10 edging sts; 1 shawl st joined.

Rep Rows 1–4 (do not rep the set-up row) 129 more times—10 edging sts rem; all shawl sts have been joined. BO rem sts.

finishing

Weave in all loose ends. Soak shawl in a basin of water. To block, pin the top edge along a straight line to about 54" (137 cm) wide. Pin the center point straight down from the middle of the top edging to measure about 24" (61 cm) long, then pin out the rem points on each side of center, forming a half-circle shape.

Galax

SHAWL

DESIGNED BY Carol Feller

With a wide, curved shape, the Galax Shawl is one versatile accessory. The sideways edging is worked modularly with increases and short-rows, creating the stitches for the future body section. This prevents picking up stitches later and makes for a smooth, lacy join between the two sections.

finished size

110" (279.5 cm) along outer edge, 70" (178 cm) along inner edge, and 11" (28 cm) wide.

yarn

Worsted (#4 Medium)

SHOWN HERE: HiKoo Kenzie (50% New Zealand merino, 25% nylon, 10% angora, 10% alpaca, 5% silk noils; 160 yd [146 m]/1¾ oz [50 g]): #1008 kale, 5 balls. Yarn distributed by Skacel.

needles

Size 8 (5 mm): 32" (80 cm) circular (cir).

Adjust needle size if necessary to obtain the correct gauge.

notions

Marker (m); tapestry needle.

gauge

17 sts and 21 rows = 4" (10 cm) in St st.

NOTES

✦ This shawl is worked back and forth in rows. A circular needle is used to accommodate the large number of stitches.

✦ The edging is worked first side to side in short-rows, with one body stitch added to the left of the marker at the end of every right-side row. Adding the body stitches in this way avoids the necessity of picking them up along the edging later, resulting in a smooth, lacy join between the two sections. Do not wrap stitches when turning.

✦ The body stitches are not included on the edging chart. There are 11 body stitches added after every 22-row repeat of the Edging chart.

shawl

EDGING

CO 20 sts.

Set-up row: (WS) Sl 1 pwise wyf, place marker, purl to end. Work Rows 1–22 of Edging chart (see Notes) 25 times, then rep Rows 1–16 once more—303 sts: 19 edging sts to right of m and 284 body sts to left of m.

Next row: (RS) BO 19 edging sts, removing m—284 body sts rem.

BODY

Work Rows 1–51 of Body chart—220 sts rem. BO all sts as foll: *P2tog, sl st from right to left needle; rep from * to end.

finishing

Weave in ends. Block.

EDGING

(blank)	k on RS; p on WS
V	sl 1 pwise wyb on RS; sl 1 pwise wyf on WS
O	yo
•	p on RS; k on WS
↻	k1f&b, then turn
/	k2tog
\	ssk
⋏	k3tog
⋏ (sl)	sl 1, k2tog, psso
4↑	k4tog
sl 1, k3tog, psso
(grey)	no stitch
☐	pattern repeat
▏	marker placement

BODY

35 st repeat

Galax shawl

Legend:

- ☐ k on RS; p on WS
- ☐ p on RS; k on WS
- ＞ sl 1 pwise wyb on RS; sl 1 pwise wyf on WS
- • sl 1 pwise wyb on RS; sl 1 pwise wyf on WS
- ＼ k2tog
- ○ yo
- ／ ssk
- ☐ no stitch
- ☐ pattern repeat

Madeleine

SHAWL

DESIGNED BY Courtney Kelley

This pretty picot-edged shawl is a great traveling or weekend project. It is knitted point to point in a garter-based bias-stitch pattern that is worked simultaneously with the picot edge. Endlessly customizable and requiring fewer than 300 yards (275 meters) of yarn, it's ideal for quick gifts and using up that odd skein or two of yarn.

finished size
About 54" (137 cm) wide and 24" (61 cm) long at point.

yarn
Worsted weight (#4 Medium).

SHOWN HERE: The Fibre Company Road to China (65% baby alpaca, 15% silk, 10% camel, 10% cashmere; 69 yd [63 ml]/50 g): jade, 4 skeins.

needles
Size U.S. 10 (6 mm).

Adjust needle size if necessary to obtain the correct gauge.

notions
Tapestry needle.

gauge
About 11 stitches and 18 rows = 4" (10 cm) in bias-stitch pattern.

shawl

CO 2 sts.

Set-up Row 1: K1f&b (see Glossary), k1—3 sts.

Set-up Row 2: [K1f&b] 2 times, k1—5 sts.

Cont to inc in patt as foll:

Row 1: Sl 1, *ssk, yo; rep from * to last 2 sts, k2.

Row 2: MP (see Stitch Guide), k1f&b, knit to end—1 st inc'd.

Row 3: Sl 1, *ssk, yo; rep from * to last 3 sts, k3.

Row 4: K1f&b, knit to end—1 st inc'd.

Rep these 4 rows 29 more times, ending with Row 4—65 sts, 30 picots; piece measures about 27" (68.5 cm) from CO.

Dec in patt as foll:

Row 1: Sl 1, k1, *yo, ssk; rep from * to last 3 sts, k3.

Row 2: MP, ssk, knit to end—1 st dec'd.

Row 3: Sl 1, k1, *yo, ssk; rep from * to last 2 sts, k2.

Row 4: Ssk, knit to end—1 st dec'd.

Rep these 4 rows 29 more times, ending with Row 4—5 sts rem.

Next row: Sl 1, k1, yo, ssk, k1.

Next row: Ssk, k3—4 sts rem.

Next row: Ssk, k2tog—2 sts rem.

BO rem 2 sts.

finishing

Weave in loose ends. Steam-block to measurements.

Lelani
Flower Motif
SHAWL

DESIGNED BY Kristin Omdahl

This generously sized, luxurious shawl is an exquisite way to add warmth and drama to any outfit. Wear this triangular shawl pinned, tied, or wrapped in the traditional methods, or lace the side triangles through the edges of the flower motifs on the opposite sides for a secure wrap that allows the edging to cascade down the front in beautiful drapes.

finished size
About 78" (198 cm) wide and 27" (68.5 cm) long.

yarn
DK weight (#3 Light).

SHOWN HERE: Blue Sky Alpaca Melange (100% baby alpaca; 110 yd [100 m]/50 g): #800 Cornflower, 5 skeins.

needles
Size U.S. 3 (3.25 mm): straight plus 1 extra needle for three-needle bind-off.

Adjust needle size if necessary to obtain the correct gauge. Exact gauge is not critical for this project.

notions
Contrasting cotton waste yarn for provisional cast-on; markers (m); tapestry needle.

gauge
16 stitches and 32 rows = 4" (10 cm) in garter stitch, after blocking. Each motif measures about 8¼" (21 cm) square, after blocking.

motif 1

CO 12 sts.

Row 1: Knit.

Row 2: *K1 wrapping the yarn 4 times around the needle, k1; rep from *.

Row 3: Sl all 12 sts to right-hand needle, dropping all extra loops, then sl these sts back to left-hand needle, then work (k1, yo, k1, yo, k1) in each st—60 sts.

Row 4: Knit.

EDGING

Note: The remainder of the motif is worked perpendicular to Row 4; the last st of every other row is knitted together with a live st from Row 4.

Set-up row: With waste yarn and WS facing, use a provisional method (see Glossary) to CO 8 sts, turn, k7, k2tog (1 edging st and 1 st from Row 4 of motif).

Row 1: K2, [yo, k2tog] 2 times, yo, k2—9 sts.

Row 2: K2, yo, k2, [yo, k2tog] 2 times, k2tog (1 edging st and 1 st from Row 4 of motif)—10 sts.

Row 3: K2, [yo, k2tog] 2 times, k2, yo, k2—11 sts.

Row 4: K2, yo, k4, [yo, k2tog] 2 times, k2tog (1 edging st and 1 st from Row 4 of motif)—12 sts.

Row 5: K2, [yo, k2tog] 2 times, k4, yo, k2—13 sts.

Row 6: K2, yo, k6, [yo, k2tog] 2 times, k2tog (1 edging st and 1 st from Row 4 of motif)—14 sts.

Row 7: K2, [yo, k2tog] 2 times, k6, yo, k2—15 sts.

Row 8: K2, yo, k8, [yo, k2tog] 2 times, k2tog (1 edging st and 1 st from Row 4 of motif)—16 sts.

Row 9: K2, [yo, k2tog] 2 times, k8, yo, k2—17 sts.

Row 10: BO 10 sts (1 st on right-hand needle), k1, [yo, k2tog] 2 times, k1—7 sts rem.

Row 11: K2, [yo, k2tog] 2 times, yo, k1f&b—9 sts.

Rows 12–20: Rep Rows 2–10 once.

Rep Rows 11–20 ten more times.

Next row: Use the three-needle method (see Glossary) to BO the last row tog with the set-up row of the edging.

Thread CO tail on tapestry needle and sew tog Rows 1 and 2 to form a circle. Fasten off. Weave in loose ends.

motif 2

Join first two petals of edging (indicated by blue and green dots on schematic) to Motif 1 at end of Edging Rows 9 and 19 as foll: Do not turn at end of row, insert right needle tip into tip of first petal of motif to be joined, yo and draw through loop—1 st. Turn work.

Next row: Sl 1, k1, psso, cont to BO 10 sts (1 st on right-hand needle), k1, [yo, k2tog] 2 times, k1—7 sts rem.

Join third petal (indicated by red dot on Construction Diagram) as foll: At end of next Edging Row 9, use the knitted method (see Glossary) to CO 4 sts, insert right needle tip in end of next petal, yo, and draw through loop, turn.

Next row: Sl 1, k1, psso, cont to BO 14 sts (the 4 new sts CO and the foll 10 sts; 1 st on right needle tip).

Note: This is the corner petal that will join four motifs in one point.

Work rem petals without joining.

When joining the next two motifs at the corner petal, CO 2 sts instead of 4, join with sl st in center of the same join st as for Motifs 1 and 2, BO 2 sts.

Work another corner join in the third join from the first corner join on Motifs 3 and 4.

Join Motif 5 to the corner join of Motifs 2, 3, and 4. Join Motif 6 to the corner join of Motifs 1, 2, and 5.

side triangles

Note: The side triangles are worked sideways. Use a marker to visually separate each triangle from the edging. The decreases are worked next to the marker on every other row.

TRIANGLE 1

Working along edge of motifs, pick up and knit 1 st in corner petal of top motif, *use the knitted method to CO 11 sts, pick up and knit 1 st in next petal; rep from * 8 more times (CO edge is joined to every petal), CO 8 more sts—117 sts total.

Set-up row: K8, place marker (pm), knit to end.

Row 1: Knit to 2 sts before m, k2tog, sl m, k2, [yo, k2tog] 2 times, yo, k2—117 sts; 108 sts rem before m, 9 sts after m.

Row 2: K2, yo, k2, [yo, k2tog] 2 times, k1, sl m, knit to end—118 sts.

Row 3: Knit to 2 sts before m, k2tog, sl m, k2, [yo, k2tog] 2 times, k2, yo, k2—118 sts; 107 sts rem before m, 11 sts after m.

Row 4: K2, yo, k4, [yo, k2tog] 2 times, k1, sl m, knit to end—119 sts.

Row 5: Knit to 2 sts before m, k2tog, sl m, k2, [yo, k2tog] 2 times, k4, yo, k2—119 sts; 106 sts rem before m, 13 sts after m.

Row 6: K2, yo, k6, [yo, k2tog] 2 times, k1, sl m, knit to end—120 sts.

Row 7: Knit to 2 sts before m, k2tog, sl m, k2, [yo, k2tog] 2 times, k6, yo, k2—120 sts; 105 sts rem before m, 15 sts after m.

Row 8: K2, yo, k8, [yo, k2tog] 2 times, k2tog, k1, sl m, knit to end—121 sts.

Row 9: Knit to 2 sts before m, k2tog, sl m, k2, [yo, k2tog] 2 times, k8, yo, k2—121 sts; 104 sts rem before m, 17 sts after m.

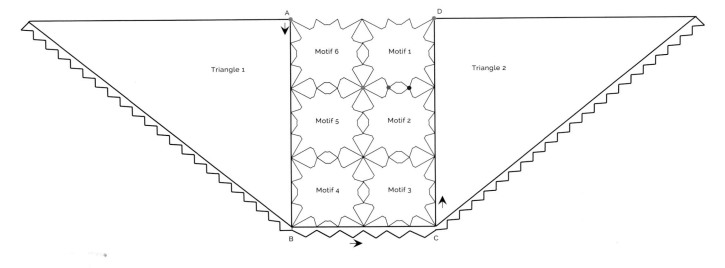

This shawl is composed of 3 sections made up of 6 motifs, 2 triangles and edging. Work each motif separately and join tips of petals as you work, beginning with Motif 2.

Triangle 1 is picked up beginning at A and working toward B, picking up stitches in the petal points and casting on stitches between points. Edging stitches are cast on using knitted cast-on.

After completing Triangle 1, return to B and pick up and k8 sts in the 8 cast-on edging stitches and work in the direction of the arrow toward C.

Triangle 2 is begun by picking up stitches in the petal points and casting on stitches between points in the direction of the arrow toward D, in the same manner as for Triangle 1.

- ● First joining of petal points
- ● Second joining of petal points
- ● Third joining of petal points

Row 10: BO 10 sts (1 st on right-hand needle), k1, [yo, k2tog] 2 times, k1, sl m, knit to end—111 sts; 7 sts before m, 104 sts after m.

Row 11: Knit to 2 sts before m, k2tog, sl m, k2, [yo, k2tog] 2 times, yo, k1f&b (see Glossary)—112 sts; 103 sts before m; 9 sts after m.

Rows 12–20: Rep Rows 2–10 once—108 sts; 99 sts before m, 9 sts after m.

Rep Rows 11–20 nineteen more times, then rep Rows 11–16 once more—15 sts rem; piece measures about 30" (76 cm) from pick-up row.

Next row: K2tog, removing m, k1, [yo, k2tog] 2 times, k6, yo, k2—15 sts.

Next row: K2, yo, k8, [yo, k2tog] 2 times, k1—16 sts.

Next row: K2, [yo, k2tog] 2 times, k8, yo, k2—17 sts.

Next row: BO 10 sts (1 st on right-hand needle), k1, [yo, k2tog] 2 times, k1—7 sts rem. Loosely BO all sts.

CENTER EDGING

Note: This edging begins from the CO edge of Triangle 1. It is worked alone along the bottom of the center motifs and is joined to the points of the center motifs at the end of every Row 10 as foll:

With RS facing, pick up and k8 in 8 sts CO at end of first triangle, turn.

Row 1: K2, [yo, k2tog] 2 times, yo, k2—9 sts.

Row 2: K2, yo, k2, [yo, k2tog] 2 times, k1—10 sts.

Row 3: K2, [yo, k2tog] 2 times, k2, yo, k2—11 sts.

Row 4: K2, yo, k4, [yo, k2tog] 2 times, k1—12 sts.

Row 5: K2, [yo, k2tog] 2 times, k4, yo, k2—13 sts.

Lelani Flower Motif shawl

Row 6: K2, yo, k6, [yo, k2tog] 2 times, k1—14 sts.

Row 7: K2, [yo, k2tog] 2 times, k6, yo, k2—15 sts.

Row 8: K2, yo, k8, [yo, k2tog] 2 times, k1—16 sts.

Row 9: Inset tip of right-hand needle into end of motif petal, k2, [yo, k2tog] 2 times, k8, yo, k2—17 sts and tip of petal.

Row 10: BO 10 sts (1 st on right-hand needle), k1, [yo, k2tog] 2 times, k2tog (1 edging st and tip of petal)—7 sts rem.

Row 11: K2, [yo, k2tog] 2 times, yo, k1f&b—9 sts.

Rows 12–20: Rep Rows 2–10 once.

Rep Rows 11–20 four more times.

TRIANGLE 2

Set-up row: At the end of the last rep of Row 10, pm, pick up and knit 1 st in corner petal (last petal joined on center edging), *use the knitted method to CO 11 sts, pick up and knit 1 st in next petal (along the vertical edge of the center motifs; see Construction Diagram); rep from * 8 more times (CO edge is joined to every petal along vertical edge of center motifs)—117 sts total.

Row 1: Knit to 2 sts before m, k2tog, sl m, k2, [yo, k2tog] 2 times, yo, k2—117 sts; 108 sts rem before m, 9 sts after m.

Row 2: K2, yo, k2, [yo, k2tog] 2 times, k1, sl m, knit to end—118 sts.

Row 3: Knit to 2 sts before m, k2tog, sl m, k2, [yo, k2tog] 2 times, k2, yo, k2—118 sts; 107 sts rem before m, 11 sts after m.

Row 4: K2, yo, k4, [yo, k2tog] 2 times, k1, sl m, knit to end—119 sts.

Row 5: Knit to 2 sts before m, k2tog, sl m, k2, [yo, k2tog] 2 times, k4, yo, k2—119 sts; 106 sts rem before m, 13 sts after m.

Row 6: K2, yo, k6, [yo, k2tog] 2 times, k1, sl m, knit to end—120 sts.

Row 7: Knit to 2 sts before m, k2tog, sl m, k2, [yo, k2tog] 2 times, k6, yo, k2—120 sts; 105 sts rem before m, 15 sts after m.

Row 8: K2, yo, k8, [yo, k2tog] 2 times, k2tog, k1, sl m, knit to end—121 sts.

Row 9: Knit to 2 sts before m, k2tog, sl m, k2, [yo, k2tog] 2 times, k8, yo, k2—121 sts; 104 sts rem before m, 17 sts after m.

Row 10: BO 10 sts (1 st on right-hand needle), k1, [yo, k2tog] 2 times, k1, sl m, knit to end—111 sts; 7 sts before m, 104 sts after m.

Row 11: Knit to 2 sts before m, k2tog, sl m, k2, [yo, k2tog] 2 times, yo, k1f&b—112 sts; 103 sts before m, 9 sts after m.

Rows 12–20: Rep Rows 2–10 once—108 sts; 99 sts before m, 9 sts after m.

Rep Rows 11–20 nineteen more times, then rep Rows 11–16 once more—15 sts rem; piece measures about 30" (76 cm) from CO edge.

Next row: K2tog, removing m, k1, [yo, k2tog] 2 times, k6, yo, k2—15 sts.

Next row: K2, yo, k8, [yo, k2tog] 2 times, k1—16 sts.

Next row: K2, [yo, k2tog] 2 times, k8, yo, k2—17 sts.

Next row: BO 10 sts (1 st on right-hand needle), k1, [yo, k2tog] 2 times, k1—7 sts rem.

Loosely BO all sts.

finishing

Weave in loose ends. Wet-block and pin to finished measurements. Let air-dry completely before removing pins.

The Return Journey

SHAWL

DESIGNED BY Lisa Shroyer

This cabled shawl starts at one corner and is worked side to side, increasing, then decreasing, at a slow rate, which creates a long, shallow triangle. I-cord edges are worked in as you go. When you arrive at the end, finishing is minimal—the journey is complete!

finished size
About 84" (213.5 cm) long and 14" (35.5 cm) deep at center.

yarn
Worsted weight (#4 Medium).

SHOWN HERE: Plymouth Worsted Merino Superwash (100% merino; 218 yd [199 m]/100 g): #7 Heather Gray, 4 skeins.

needles
Size U.S. 7 (4.5 mm): 24" (60 cm) or longer circular (cir).

Adjust needle size if necessary to obtain the correct gauge.

notions
Waste yarn for provisional cast-on; tapestry needle; cable needle (cn).

gauge
15 stitches of charted pattern repeat = 2½" (6.5 cm) wide; 29 rows in pattern = 4" (10 cm) high.

STITCH GUIDE

I-cord Edging
(worked over 3 sts at each edge)

Row 1: (RS) With yarn held in back (wyb), sl 3 sts pwise; pull yarn taut across WS and work in patt to last 3 sts, k3.

Row 2: (WS) With yarn held in front (wyf), sl 3 sts pwise; pull yarn taut across front of work and work in patt to last 3 sts, p3.

Rep Rows 1 and 2 throughout for patt.

1 over 1 Left Cross (1/1 LC)
Sl 1 to cn and hold in front, k1 tbl, k1 tbl from cn.

1 over 1 Right Cross (1/1 RC)
Sl 1 to cn and hold in back, k1 tbl, k1 tbl from cn.

(1 over 1 Left Purl Cross (1/1 LPC)
Sl 1 to cn and hold in front, p1, k1 tbl from cn.

1 over 1 Right Purl Cross (1/1 RPC)
Sl 1 to cn and hold in back, k1 tbl, p1 from cn.

2 over 2 Left Purl Cross (2/2 LPC)
Sl 2 to cn and hold in front, (k1 tbl) twice, sl sts on cn to left needle tip, sl knit st from left needle tip to cn and hold in front, p1 from left needle, k1 tbl from cn.

2 over 2 Right Purl Cross (2/2 RPC)
Sl 2 to cn and hold in back, sl purl st on left needle tip to right needle tip, then to right needle tip of cn, k1 tbl from left needle, (p1, [k1 tbl] twice) from cn.

1 over 2 Left Purl Cross Decrease (1/2 LPC dec)
Sl 1 to right needle tip, sl 1 to cn and hold in front, sl st from right needle tip back to left needle tip, p2tog, k1 tbl from cn.

NOTES

✤ This shawl is worked side to side and features shaping along the right-hand edge to create a triangle.

✤ The edges are worked in a three-stitch I-cord pattern. These stitches are not shown on the charts, but the edge pattern should be worked throughout.

shawl

Use the invisible provisional method (see Glossary) to CO 3 sts. Work 4 rows in I-cord (see Glossary).

Next row: With RS still facing, turn work 90 degrees clockwise and use right needle tip to pick up and knit 3 sts along side of I-cord; carefully remove waste yarn from CO and place 3 live sts on left needle, then knit these 3 sts—9 sts total.

Next row: (WS) P3, work Row 1 of Chart A over 3 sts, p3.

Next row: (RS) Work 3 sts in I-cord edging patt (see Stitch Guide), work Row 2 of Chart A, work last 3 sts in I-cord edging patt.

Next row: (WS) Work 3 sts in edging patt, work Row 3 of chart, work 3 sts in edging patt.

Cont to work edge sts in patt (see Notes) and work in charted patt through Row 63—24 sts total; 6 edge sts + 18 body sts. Work Rows 64–123 four times, working full reps according to red rep box—84 sts: 6 edge sts + 78 body sts; piece should measure about 42" (106.5 cm) from bottom.

SHAPE SECOND HALF

Work Rows 1–60 of Chart B four times, working full reps according to red rep box—24 sts rem: 6 edge sts + 18 body sts. Work Rows 61–120 once—9 sts rem: 6 edge sts + 3 body sts.

Next row: (RS) Sl 3 sts wyb, k3tog, sl 4 sts back to left needle, pull yarn taut across WS, k2, ssk, sl 3 sts back to left needle, *k3, sl 3 sts back to left needle and pull yarn taut across WS; rep from * once more—6 sts rem.

Break the yarn and thread the tail onto the tapestry needle. Arrange sts on needle tips—3 sts each tip—and, with RS facing, use Kitchener st (see Glossary) to graft edges together.

finishing

Weave in all ends. Block piece to finished measurements.

CHART A

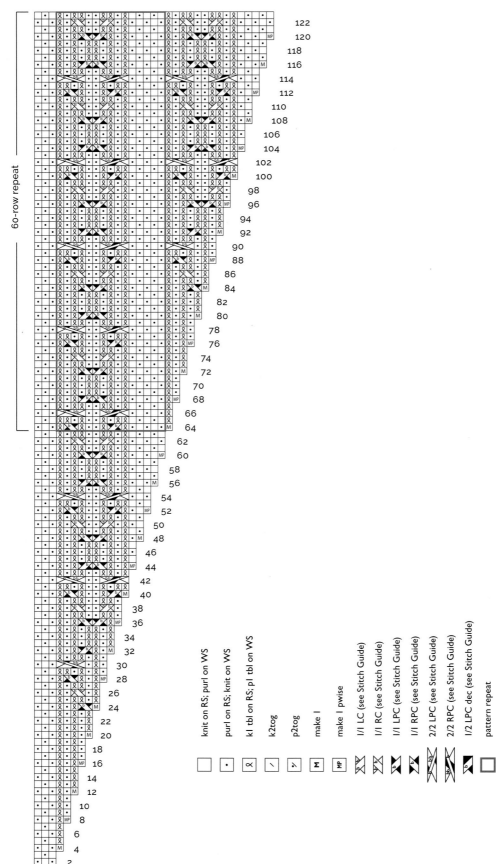

knit on RS; purl on WS

purl on RS; knit on WS

k1 tbl on RS; p1 tbl on WS

k2tog

p2tog

make 1

make 1 pwise

1/1 LC (see Stitch Guide)

1/1 RC (see Stitch Guide)

1/1 LPC (see Stitch Guide)

1/1 RPC (see Stitch Guide)

2/2 LPC (see Stitch Guide)

2/2 RPC (see Stitch Guide)

1/2 LPC dec (see Stitch Guide)

pattern repeat

Wheeled Lace

SHAWL

DESIGNED BY Kristin Omdahl

Designer Kristin Omdahl takes a circular twist on traditional lacy shawl patterns. The all-over medallion pattern makes for an airy fabric, and the delicate matching edging is a striking additional detail that is sure to turn heads.

finished size
60" (152.5 cm) wide × 30" (76 cm) tall at center.

yarn
Laceweight (#0 Lace)

SHOWN HERE: Shibui Knits Silk Cloud (60% kid mohair, 40% silk; 330 yd [300 m]/⅞ oz [25 g]): #SC350 storm, 2 skeins.

needles
Size 6 (4 mm): 24" (60 cm) or longer circular (cir) and set of 2 double-pointed (dpn).

Adjust needle size if necessary to obtain the correct gauge.

notions
Markers (m); tapestry needle; pins for blocking.

gauge
16 sts and 16 rows = 4" (10 cm) in patt, after blocking.

shawl

CO 17 sts. Do not join.

Next row: (WS) K1, place marker (pm), k7, pm, k1, pm, k7, pm, k1. Next row: K1, sl m, work Row 1 of Medallion chart to m, sl m, k1, sl m, work Row 1 of chart to m, sl m, k1—21 sts.

Cont in patt (keeping first, center, and last st in garter st), work Rows 2–16 of chart once, then work Rows 17–32 six times, adding one more 16-st rep on each side each time—241 sts. *Note:* Remove m on next row.

Next row: (RS) K1, yo, knit to m, yo, k1, yo, knit to last st, yo, k1—245 sts.

Knit 1 WS row. BO all sts.

finishing

Block shawl to 56" wide at upper edge and 28" tall at center, pinning lower V edge at every medallion, between every medallion, at center point, and at 2 side points (beg and end of BO row)—33 pins. Pin as desired along top edge. Pinned points along lower V edge serve as guides for joining medallion edging. Edging: With dpn, CO 3 sts. Do not join.

Row 1: (RS) K1f&b, yo, k2—5 sts.

Rows 2, 4, 8, and 10: Knit.

Row 3: K2, yo, k1, yo, k2—7 sts.

Row 5: K2, yo, k3, yo, k2, pick up and knit 1 st in point at lower edge of shawl—10 sts.

Row 6: K2tog, knit to end—9 sts rem.

Row 7: K1, ssk, yo, s2kp2 (see Stitch Guide), yo, k2tog, k1—7 sts rem.

Row 9: K1, ssk, yo, k3tog, k1—5 sts rem.

Row 11: Ssk, k1, k2tog—3 sts rem.

Row 12: P3tog—1 st rem.

Row 13: Knit into front, back, and front of same st—3 sts.

Row 14: Knit.

Rep Rows 1–14 thirty-one more times, then work Rows 1–12 once more—33 medallions, each joined to lower edge of shawl at one of 33 points created in blocking shawl. Fasten off last st. Steam-block medallion edging to flatten medallions. Weave in ends.

16-st repeat

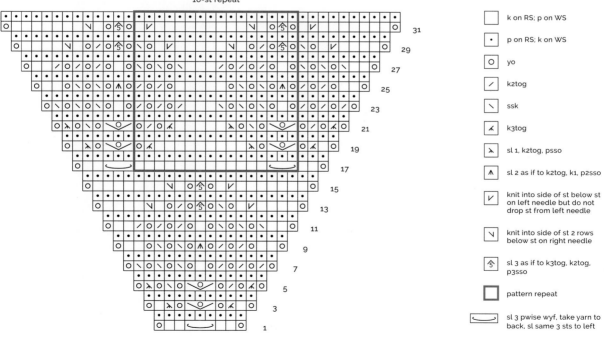

	k on RS; p on WS
•	p on RS; k on WS
O	yo
/	k2tog
\	ssk
⋏	k3tog
⋏	sl 1, k2tog, psso
⋏	sl 2 as if to k2tog, k1, p2sso
V	knit into side of st below st on left needle but do not drop st from left needle
⋁	knit into side of st 2 rows below st on right needle
⬆	sl 3 as if to k3tog, k2tog, p3sso
☐	pattern repeat
⌣	sl 3 pwise wyf, take yarn to back, sl same 3 sts to left

Impasto
SHAWLETTE

DESIGNED BY Susanna IC

The colorwork in this shawl was inspired by the rich golden hues of fields ripening beneath the blue summer sky. Designer Susanna IC chose a simple slip-stitch pattern to create an effect that looks good on both sides and is lacy enough to drape well if knitted on larger needles.

finished size
76" (193 cm) wide, 16" (40.5 cm) high at center, and 8" (20.5 cm) high at each end, after blocking.

yarn
DK (#3 Light)

SHOWN HERE: Berroco Pure Pima (100% pima cotton; 115 yd [105 ml/50 g): #2246 delft (MC, light blue), 2 skeins; #2205 jojoba (yellow), #2206 curry (gold), #2237 olive, and #2263 Caneel Bay (dark blue), 1 skein each.

needles
Size 10 (6 mm): 40" (100 cm) circular (cir).

Adjust needle size if necessary to obtain the correct gauge.

notions
Tapestry needle, blocking pins.

gauge
15 sts and 18 rows = 4" (10 cm) in St st; 15 sts and 23 rows = 4" (10 cm) in slip st patt.

Make Loop (ML)
Insert right needle tip into the st 2 rows below the next st on left needle and draw up an elongated loop on the right needle. Knit the next st, then pass the elongated loop over the knit st.

Slip-Stitch Pattern:
(multiple of 4 sts + 5)

Set-up row: (WS) With yellow, p2, p1 wrapping yarn twice around needle, *p3, p1 wrapping yarn twice around needle; rep from * to last 2 sts, p2; do not rep the set-up row. *Note:* Work each 4-row rep using colors in the order given in the directions.

Row 1: (RS) K2, *sl 1 double-wrapped st as if to purl with yarn in back (pwise wyb) dropping extra wrap, k1, ML (see above), k1; rep from * to last 3 sts, sl 1 double-wrapped st pwise wyb dropping extra wrap, k2.

Row 2: P2, sl 1 as if to purl with yarn in front (pwise wyf), *p3, sl 1 pwise wyf; rep from * to last 2 sts, p2.

Row 3: Knit.

Row 4: P2, p1 wrapping yarn twice around needle, *p3, p1 wrapping yarn twice around needle; rep from * to last 2 sts, p2.

Rep Rows 1–4 for patt, changing to a new color at the start of Row 1 for each rep.

NOTES

✣ The shawl is deliberately worked using larger needles at a looser gauge than is usual for this yarn.

✣ The piece begins at the lower edge of the colorwork section. After completing the slip-stitch pattern, the solid-color section is shaped into a narrow curve using decreases and short-rows.

✣ Do not wrap the stitches at the short-row turning points. The turning gaps are closed by working the stitches on each side of the gap together as either ssk or p2tog. This simultaneously shapes the curve and decreases the number of stitches.

shawl

With yellow, loosely CO 321 sts. Purl 1 WS row, then knit 1 RS row. With yellow, work Set-up row of slip st patt (see Stitch Guide). Cont in slip st patt, work 4 rows of each color in this order, ending with Row 4 of patt: gold, olive, dark blue, light blue, yellow, gold, olive, dark blue—33 slip st patt rows completed, including set-up row. With light blue, work Rows 1–3 of patt, ending with a RS row—36 slip st patt rows and 38 rows total completed; piece measures about 6¾" (17 cm) from CO. Cont with light blue to end. Purl 1 WS row.

Dec row: (RS) Ssk, *k5, sl 2 as if to k2tog, k1, p2sso; rep from * to last 7 sts, k5, k2tog—241 sts rem. Purl 1 WS row. Shape crescent section using short-rows and decs (see Notes) as foll:

Short-row 1: (RS) K127, turn.

Short-row 2: (WS) P13, turn.

Short-row 3: K12, work next 2 sts (1 st from each side of turning gap) tog as ssk, k5, turn—1 st dec'd.

Short-row 4: P17, work next 2 sts (1 st from each side of turning gap) tog as p2tog, p5, turn—1 st dec'd.

Short-row 5: K22, ssk sts on each side of gap, k5, turn—1 st dec'd.

Short-row 6: P27, p2tog sts on each side of gap, p5, turn—1 st dec'd.

Short-rows 7–40: Cont in this manner, working 5 more sts in each row before dec to close gap, then work 5 more sts after the dec, then turn—203 sts rem; no sts rem unworked before turning at the ends of Short-rows 39 and 40.

BO all sts in 1×1 rib.

finishing

Weave in ends. Block to measurements, coaxing the CO edge into scalloped points.

Lale
SHAWL

DESIGNED BY Corrina Ferguson

Worked in DK yarn, this shawl starts with center counterpane, then edges are added to form a triangle. The result is a beautiful large shawl featuring a panel of lace you'll be proud to show off in any weather.

finished size
Size 32" (81.5 cm) deep and 64" (162.5 cm) wide, after blocking.

yarn
DK (#3 Light)

SHOWN HERE: Madelinetosh Tosh DK (100% merino; 225 yd [206 m]/100 g): wood violet, 3 skeins.

needles
Size 8 (5 mm): 40" (100 cm) circular (cir) needle and set of 5 double-pointed needles (dpn).

notions
Markers (m); stitch holders or waste yarn; yarn needle.

gauge
12 sts and 17 rows = 4" (10 cm) in garter st, blocked.

shawl

COUNTERPANE

CO 8 sts, divided evenly over 4 dpn. Place marker (pm) and join in the rnd. Work Rnds 1–15 of Counterpane chart—56 sts: 14 sts on each needle.

Rnd 16: Remove rnd m, sl 2, pm for new beg of rnd, knit to end of rnd.

Work Rnds 17–67 of chart, changing to circular needle when necessary—256 sts. Beg working back and forth in rows as foll:

Next row: (RS) K63, then using the backward-loop method, CO 7 sts, turn.

Next row: (WS) K8 (for lower edging), pm, k62, remove rnd m, k1, pm (for upper edging), k1, CO 3 sts, place next 64 sts on waste yarn for right wing, and rem 127 sts on another length of waste yarn for lower edging—75 sts rem.

LEFT WING

Note: The stitch counts on the upper and lower edgings will fluctuate, but will always return to the original number.

Row 1: (RS) BO 2 sts, k1, sl m, k1, ssk, knit to 3 sts before m, k2tog, k1, sl m, k1, yo 2 times, k2tog, k5—2 sts dec'd between m.

Row 2: K7, p1, knit to last st, yo 2 times, k1.

Row 3: K2, p1, knit to end.

Row 4: Knit.

Row 5: BO 2 sts, k1, sl m, k1, ssk, knit to 3 sts before m, k2tog, k1, sl m, k1, [yo 2 times, k2tog] 2 times, k4—2 sts dec'd between m.

Row 6: K6, p1, k2, p1, knit to last st, yo 2 times, k1.

Row 7: K2, p1, knit to end.

Row 8: BO 3 sts, knit to end.

Rep Rows 1–8 thirteen more times, then work Rows 1–4 once more—18 sts rem: 9 sts for upper edging, 5 sts between m, and 4 sts for lower edging. Remove m. Work Rows 1–22 of Left Wing Tip chart—4 sts rem. BO all sts.

NOTES

❖ This shawl is worked in four sections: The center counterpane, the left wing, the lower edging, then the right wing.

❖ The counterpane is worked circularly from the center out; all the other sections are worked back and forth.

LOWER EDGING

RIGHT WING TIP

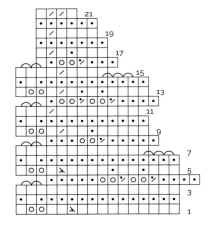

LEFT WING TIP

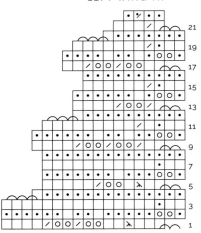

	k on RS; p on WS
•	p on RS; k on WS
℅	k1tbl
O	yo
②	yo 2 times (counts as 1 st)
/	k2tog on RS
\	ssk
↘	k2tog on WS
/	knit last st of lower edging tog with 1 st of shawl body
⅄	sl 1, k2tog, psso
⋀	sl 2 as if to k2tog, k1, p2sso
V	sl 1 pwise wyf on WS
⅃	k1f&b
v	[k1, p1, k1] into double yo—3 sts from 1 st
⌒	bind off 1 st
▨	no stitch
☐	pattern repeat

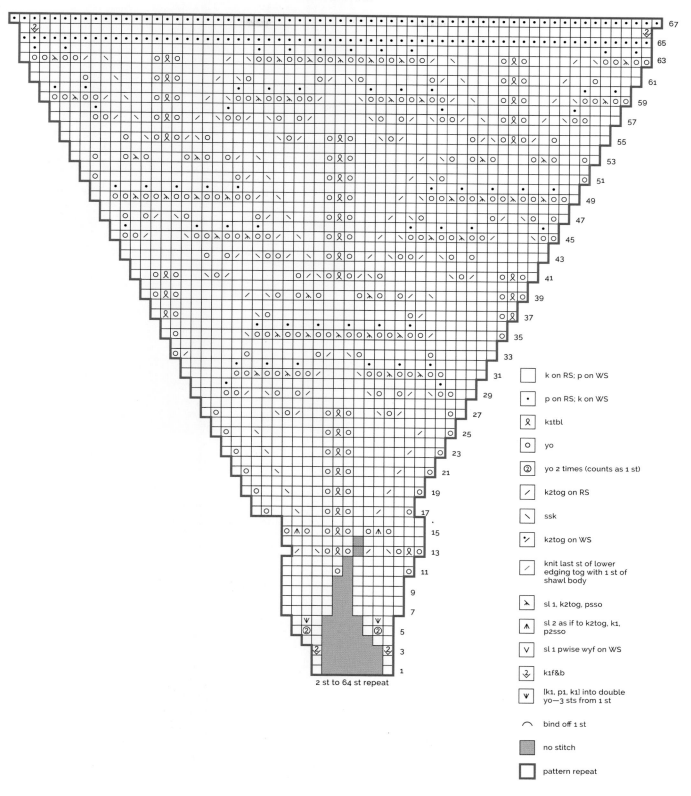

2 st to 64 st repeat

	k on RS; p on WS
	p on RS; k on WS
ℓ	k1tbl
o	yo
②	yo 2 times (counts as 1 st)
/	k2tog on RS
\	ssk
⌄	k2tog on WS
/	knit last st of lower edging tog with 1 st of shawl body
⋋	sl 1, k2tog, psso
∧	sl 2 as if to k2tog, k1, p2sso
V	sl 1 pwise wyf on WS
⤓	k1f&b
⩔	[k1, p1, k1] into double yo—3 sts from 1 st
⌒	bind off 1 st
▨	no stitch
□	pattern repeat

Lower Edging: Transfer lower 127 sts to cir needle, marking the center st. With WS facing, pick up and knit 9 sts along CO edge of lower edging of left wing—136 sts. Work Rows 1–8 of Lower Edging chart 15 times, then work Rows 1–6 once more—64 body sts rem, and next st to be worked is marked center st. Work in chart patt for 4 more rows, ending with chart Row 2, and joining edging sts to body by picking up 2 extra loops before marked center st. Work Row 3 of chart, joining last edging st to marked center st, removing m. Work in chart patt for 5 more rows, joining edging sts to body by picking up 2 extra loops after center st, ending with Row 8 of chart—63 body sts rem. Rep Rows 1–8 of Lower Edging chart 15 times, then work Rows 1–6 once more—9 edging sts rem.

RIGHT WING

Transfer rem 64 sts to needle—73 sts: 9 sts for lower edging and 64 sts for right wing.

Next row: (RS) Work Row 7 of Lower Edging chart, pm, k63, pm, pick up and knit 1 st, yo 2 times, pick up and knit 1 st—76 sts.

Next row: (WS) K1, p1, knit to end.

Row 1: (RS) K9, sl m, k1, ssk, knit to 3 sts before m, k2tog, k1, sl m, k4—2 sts dec'd between m.

Row 2: BO 2 sts, k1, sl m, knit to m, sl m, k1, [yo 2 times, k2tog] 2 times, k4.

Row 3: K5, p1, k2, p1, knit to last st, yo 2 times, k1.

Row 4: K1, p1, knit to end.

Row 5: BO 3 sts, knit to m, sl m, k1, ssk, knit to 3 sts before m, k2tog, k1, sl m, knit to end—2 sts dec'd between m.

Row 6: BO 2 sts, k1, sl m, knit to m, sl m, k1, yo 2 times, k2tog, k5.

Row 7: K6, p1, knit to last st, yo 2 times, k1.

Row 8: K1, p1, knit to end.

Rep Rows 1–8 thirteen more times, then work Rows 1–6 once more—16 sts rem: 9 sts for upper edging, 5 sts between m, and 2 sts for lower edging. Remove m. Work Rows 1–21 of Right Wing Tip chart—4 sts rem. BO all sts.

finishing

Weave in ends. Using wires or pins, wet-block shawl, making sure to pull out the points on the bottom edge and the loops on the top.

The Purple

SHAWL

DESIGNED BY Andrea Jurgrau

To create this pattern, Andrea Jurgrau started with a small doily pattern from a 1922 DMC publication that is in the public domain. She deconstructed the charts and made design adjustments, resulting in this truly vintage-inspired shawl.

finished size

This shawl measures about 38" (96.5 cm) wide and 16" (40.5 cm) long at center back, blocked; about 36" (91.5 cm) wide and 14" (35.5 cm) long at center back, after relaxing.

yarn

Fingering weight (#1 Super Fine).

SHOWN HERE: *Gradient Shawl:* Lara's Creations Majestic Entrée ColourWave (50% silk, 50% merino; 430 yd [393 ml/100 g]): "Your Highness," 1 skein.

Solid Shawl: Cascade Yarns Heritage Silk (85% merino, 15% silk; 437 yd [400 ml/100 g]): #5625 Purple Hyacinth, 1 skein.

needles

U.S. size 5 (3.75 mm): 32" (80 cm) circular (cir).

Adjust needle size if necessary to obtain the correct gauge.

notions

12" (30.5 cm) smooth waste yarn for provisional cast-on; size 14 (0.75 mm) steel crochet hook for placing beads; 12 g of Japanese 8/0 Delica beads in color 906 Purple Lined Crystal (for one shawl); size 1 (2.75 mm) steel crochet hook for bind-off; tapestry needle; flexible blocking wires; T-pins.

gauge

11 sts and 14 rows = 2" (5 cm) according to Purple Shawl chart, relaxed after blocking.

shawl

Using a provisional method (see Glossary), CO 3 sts.

Knit 15 rows—7 garter ridges. Do not turn work after the last row.

Rotate work 90 degrees and pick up and purl (see Glossary) 7 sts evenly spaced along selvedge (1 st in each garter ridge), carefully remove waste yarn from provisional CO and knit the 3 exposed sts—13 sts total.

Knitting the first 3 and last 3 sts of every row, adding beads with smaller crochet hook when specified (see page 41), work Rows 1–90 of Purple Shawl Chart—405 sts.

With larger crochet hook, use the gathered crochet method (see Glossary) to BO as foll: gather 3, chain 8, [gather 4, chain 8] 2 times, gather 3, chain 8, *[gather 4, chain 8] 4 times, gather 3, chain 8; rep from * 19 more times, [gather 4, chain 8] 2 times, gather 3.

Cut yarn, leaving a 9" (23 cm) tail. Pull tail through rem loop to secure.

finishing

Weave in loose ends to but do not trim tails.

Soak in cool water for at least 30 minutes. Roll in a towel to remove excess water.

Weave flexible blocking wires into garter bumps along straight top edge. Place on flat padded surface and pin out each crochet loop to finished dimensions.

Allow to air-dry thoroughly before removing wires and pins.

Trim tails on woven-in ends.

NOTES

✦ A circular needle is used to accommodate the large number of stitches. Do not join; work back and forth in rows.

✦ Beads are applied with smaller crochet hook (see page 41).

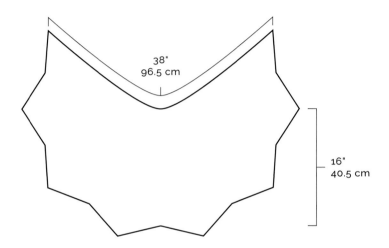

38"
96.5 cm

16"
40.5 cm

PURPLE SHAWL CHART

☐	knit on RS; purl on WS
•	purl on RS; knit on WS
○	yo
ຊ	k1tbl on RS; p1tbl on WS
M	M1 without twist (see page 24)
╱	k2tog
╲	ssk
♠	s2kp, place bead
⋀	s2kp
●	place bead
↘	sssk
↙	k3tog
⬆	gather 3
⬆	gather 4
0	crochet chain
▨	no stitch
☐	pattern repeat

6 times

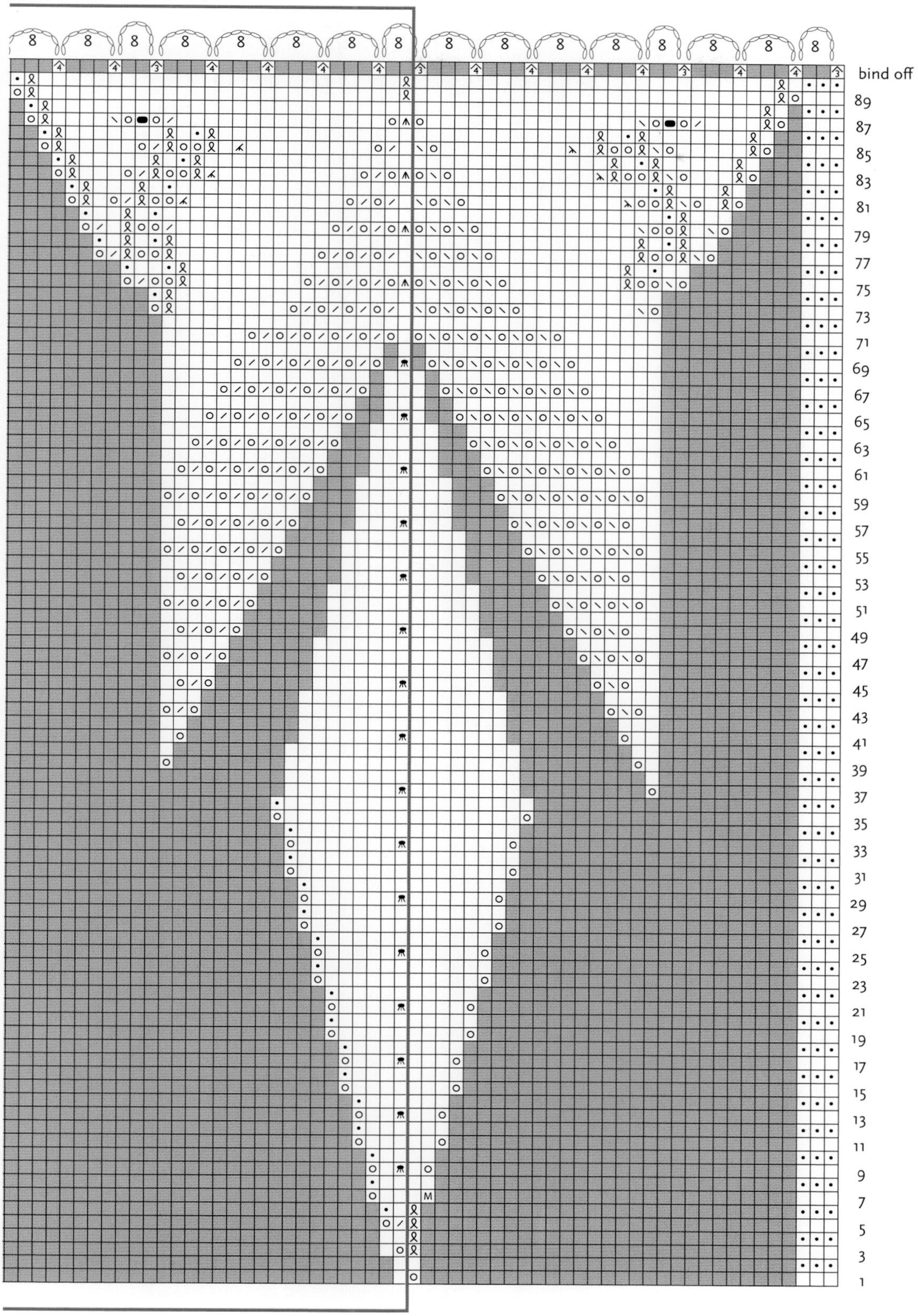
bind off
89
87
85
83
81
79
77
75
73
71
69
67
65
63
61
59
57
55
53
51
49
47
45
43
41
39
37
35
33
31
29
27
25
23
21
19
17
15
13
11
9
7
5
3
1

Darjeeling
SHAWL

DESIGNED BY Joan Forgione

For this shawl, ornate Shetland-style lace trim dresses up a simple garter-stitch triangle. The picked-up and knitted lace border and a knitted-on edging that has lace patterning on both sides creates a delicate openness, and hand-dyed silk lends sumptuous drape.

finished size
About 49" wide and 20" long.

yarn
Fingering weight (#1 Super Fine)

SHOWN HERE: Vijay Fibers Serenade (100% silk; 410 yd [375 ml]/3½ oz [100 g]): polar purple, 2 skeins.

needles
Size 6 (4 mm): 40" (100 cm) circular (cir).

Adjust needle size if necessary to obtain the correct gauge.

notions
Markers (m); tapestry needle; safety pin or removable m.

gauge
18 sts and 38 rows = 4" (10 cm) in garter st.

shawl

INNER TRIANGLE

CO 1 st.

Next row: (WS) Yo, k1—2 sts.

Next row: (RS) Yo, knit to end—1 st inc'd.

Rep last row every row 142 more times, ending with a RS row—145 sts; 72 yo loops each side.

Loosely BO all sts, pull skein through last loop but do not break yarn.

With WS facing, pick up and knit 1 st in each of 72 yo loops along edge of shawl, 1 st in CO st, and 1 st in each of 72 yo loops along other edge—145 sts. Knit 2 rows.

LACE PANEL

Next row: (RS) [K1, yo] 2 times, place marker (pm), work Row 1 of Lace Panel chart over 141 sts, pm, [yo, k1] 2 times—149 sts.

Next row: (WS) Knit.

Next row: [K1, yo] 2 times, knit to m, sl m, work chart patt to m, sl m, knit to last 2 sts, [yo, k1] 2 times—4 sts inc'd.

Next row: Knit. Rep last 2 rows until Rows 1–8 of chart have been worked a total of 3 times—193 sts.

EDGING

Next row: (RS) Knit.

Next row: (WS) Knit to end, then using the backward-loop method (see Glossary), CO 15 sts—208 sts: 15 edging sts and 193 shawl sts.

Next row: Work Row 1 of Edging chart over 15 sts, working last st of edging tog with 1 shawl st—1 shawl st dec'd.

Cont in patt until Rows 1–6 of Edging chart have been worked 64 times—16 sts rem: 15 edging sts and 1 shawl st. Loosely BO all sts.

finishing

Weave in ends. Block.

NOTES

✤ The inner garter-stitch triangle of the shawl is worked first. Then, yarnover loops are picked up and the lace panel is worked along two sides of the triangle. Finally, shawl stitches are bound off as the lace edging is worked by knitting one stitch from the edging together with one stitch from the shawl body.

✤ When working the inner triangle, it may be helpful to mark the right side of the work with a safety pin or removable marker.

LACE PANEL

6-st repeat

LACE EDGING

15 sts

☐	k on RS
•	k on WS
O	yo
╱	k2tog
╲	ssk
⋀	sl 2 sts as if to k2tog, k1, p2sso—2 sts dec'd
⩘	k2tog on WS
⩗	ssk on WS
V	sl 1 pwise wyb
⧄	k1f&b
╱	k2tog (last st of edging tog with 1 shawl st)
⌐∿	BO 4 sts
⌐	st rem on right needle after BO
☐	pattern repeat

Trillium

SHAWL

DESIGNED BY Manda Shah

Work the generous half-circle Trillium Shawl from the top down and finish with a dramatic perpendicular edging. The semicircular shape is achieved with six increases worked within the lace patterning across each fourth row.

finished size

72" (*183 cm) wide and 33½" (85 cm) tall.

yarn

Fingering weight (#1 Super Fine)

SHOWN HERE: Anzula Squishy (80% superwash merino wool, 10% cashmere, 10% nylon; 385 yd [352 m]/4 oz [115 g]): madam, 2 skeins.

needles

Size 6 (4 mm): 32" (80 cm) circular (cir) and set of double-pointed (dpn).

Adjust needle size if necessary to obtain the correct gauge.

notions

Tapestry needle.

gauge

17 sts and 27 rows = 4" (10 cm) in Leaf Lace patt, after blocking.

shawl

With cir needle and using the knitted method, CO 5 sts. Do not join.

Row 1: (RS) K2, yo, k1, yo, k2—7 sts.

Row 2: (WS) K2, p3, k2.

Row 3: K2, yo, k3, yo, k2—9 sts.

Row 4: K2, p5, k2.

Row 5: K2, yo, [k1, yo] 5 times, k2—15 sts.

Row 6: K2, p11, k2.

Row 7: K15.

Row 8: K2, p11, k2.

Row 9: K2, [work Leaf Lace Set-up chart over 3 sts (inc'd to 5 sts), k1] 3 times, k1—21 sts.

Keeping first and last 2 sts in garter st and st between charts in St st, cont in patt through Row 36 of chart—69 sts.

Next row: (RS) K2, [work Leaf Lace chart over 21 sts (inc'd to 23 sts), k1] 3 times, k1—75 sts.

Keeping first and last 2 sts in garter st and st between charts in St st, cont in patt until chart has been worked 5 times—279 sts. Break yarn.

LEAF LACE SET-UP

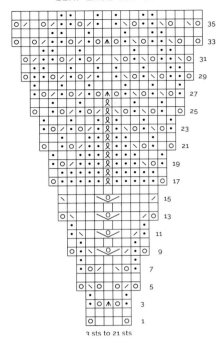

3 sts to 21 sts

	k on RS; p on WS
	p on RS; k on WS
	k1tbl on RS; p1tbl on WS
	yo
	k2tog on RS
	ssk on RS
	k2tog on WS
	ssk on WS
	sl 1 kwise, k2tog, psso
	sl 2 as if to k2tog, k1, p2sso
	(k1, yo, k1) in same st
	transfer 1 body st to left needle, k2tog on RS; p2tog (last edging st and 1 body st) on WS
	bind off 1 st
	st rem on right needle after last BO st
	no stitch
	pattern repeat

EDGING

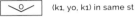

14 sts to 23 sts to 14 sts

NOTES

✤ This shawl is worked in two parts—main body and lace edge—and has a distinct right and wrong side.

✤ The main body is worked back and forth from the top down in the Leaf Lace pattern starting at the center, forming a half-circle shape. The half-circle shape is achieved by increasing the stitch count by 6 stitches every 4th row.

✤ A lace edging is worked on the perimeter of this semicircle, joined as it is being worked.

✤ A circular needle is used to work the main body to accommodate the large number of stitches.

LEAF LACE

14 st repeat

EDGING

With dpn and using the knitted method, CO 14 sts. Work Rows 1–8 of Edging chart 35 times, beg joining to body at end opposite yarn tail (end of RS row on body)—no body sts rem. (*Note*: On last rep of chart, there will be no body st left to join on last row.) BO all sts.

finishing

Weave in ends. Block.

Note: This shawl requires severe blocking. It will not block properly if the lace edge is worked too tight or does not have enough joins. To create a well blocked shawl, follow these tips:

1 Work more joins. If the pattern calls for 1:1 join, try 2:3 ratio, i.e. 3 rows of edge over 2 live stitches.

2 For lace edge only, use knitting needles one size larger than those used for shawl body.

3 Double block the shawl. Work the shawl body and block it with live stitches, then work the lace edge with enough joins to keep the shawl shape intact. Re-block the whole shawl again.

Lindsay

SHAWL

DESIGNED BY Tabetha Hedrick

Tabetha Hedrick was inspired by the legacy of pioneer women in the Rocky Mountains when she designed this shawl, which has a sweet, vintage appeal and streamlined patterning. Two colors of a sock yarn alternate within simple lace bands.

finished size
About 77½" (197 cm) wide and 16" (40.5 cm) deep.

yarn
Fingering weight (#1 Super Fine).

SHOWN HERE: Shibui Knits Staccato (65% superwash merino, 30% silk, 5% nylon; 191 yd [175 ml/50 g): #115 Chrome (MC), 2 skeins; #165 Poodle Skirt (CC), 1 skein.

needles
Size U.S. 6 (4 mm): 24" (60 cm) circular (cir).

Adjust needle size if necessary to obtain the correct gauge.

notions
Tapestry needle.

gauge
16 stitches and 36 rows = 4" (10 cm) in stockinette stitch.

shawl

With MC, CO 363 sts. Work Rows 1–8 of the
Lace chart once. Change to CC and work
Rows 1–8 of the chart once more. Rep last 16
rows once more, changing colors with each
8-row rep. Change to MC and knit 4 rows,
ending with a WS row. Work in short-rows
without wrapping sts as foll:

Next row: (RS) K186, turn.

Row 2: P9, turn.

Row 3: K8, ssk, k3, turn—1 st dec'd.

Row 4: P11, p2tog, p3, turn—1 st dec'd.

Row 5: Knit to 1 st before last turn, ssk, k3,
turn—1 st dec'd.

Row 6: Purl to 1 st before last turn, p2tog, p3,
turn—1 st dec'd.

Rep last 2 rows 36 more times—25 sts rem on
each side outside turning points.

Row 1: (RS) Knit to 1 st before last turn, ssk,
k4, turn—1 st dec'd.

Row 2: (WS) Purl to 1 st before last turn,
p2tog, p4, turn—1 st dec'd.

Rep last 2 rows 4 more times—277 sts rem.
Change to CC and knit 5 rows. BO all sts
loosely.

finishing

Weave in all ends. Block piece to finished
measurements.

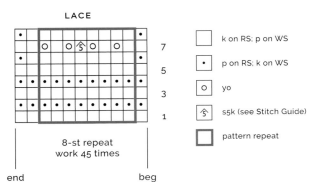

LACE

7

5

3

1

8-st repeat
work 45 times

end

beg

☐ k on RS; p on WS

• p on RS; k on WS

○ yo

⤼ s5k (see Stitch Guide)

☐ pattern repeat

Rhoeas

SHAWL

DESIGNED BY Mercedes Tarasovich

Horseshoe lace edges a generous garter-stitch triangle on this large, lofty accessory. Worked in a worsted wool-cotton blend on size U.S. 9 (5.5 mm) needles, the knitting goes quickly, and self-fringe makes for faster finishing.

finished size

About 76" (193 cm) wide and 18" (45.5 cm) deep, not including fringe.

yarn

Worsted weight (#4 Medium).

SHOWN HERE: Spud & Chloë Sweater (55% superwash wool, 45% organic cotton; 160 yd [146 ml/100 g): #7501 Popsicle, 4 skeins.

needles

Size U.S. 9 (5.5 mm): 24" (60 cm) circular (cir).

Adjust needle size if necessary to obtain the correct gauge.

notions

Markers (m); tapestry needle.

gauge

15 stitches and 27 rows = 4" (10 cm) in garter stitch.

shawl

CO 9 sts.

SET-UP

Row 1: (WS) K1, place marker (pm), p1, pm, k2, pm, p5.

Row 2: (RS) K5, sl m, k2, lifted inc right slant (see Glossary), k1, sl m, M1, k1—2 sts inc'd.

Row 3 and all WS rows: Knit to m, sl m, purl to m, sl m, k2, sl m, p5.

Row 4: K5, sl m, k2, sl m, lifted inc right slant, knit to m, sl m, knit to end—1 st inc'd.

Row 6: K5, sl m, k2, sl m, lifted inc right slant, knit to m, sl m, M1, knit to end—2 sts inc'd.

Rows 8–17: Work Rows 4–7 twice more, then Rows 4–5 once more—21 sts.

On last row, remove second and third markers, leaving the first marker between garter sts and lace patt—16 sts in lace section and 5 sts in garter st section.

BODY

Next row: Work Lace Edging chart over 16 sts, sl m, knit to end.

Work 1 more row in patt, working edging sts according to chart.

INCREASES

Inc row: (RS) Work the Lace Edging chart to m, sl m, M1, knit to end—1 st inc'd.

Work Inc row every 4th row 53 more times—75 sts; piece should measure about 37" (94 cm) from bottom. Work even in patt for 8 rows.

DECREASES

Dec row: (RS) Work Lace Edging chart to m, sl m, k2tog, knit to end—1 st dec'd.

Work Dec row every 4th row 53 more times, ending with a WS row—21 sts rem.

END SHAWL

Row 1: (RS) K5, pm, k2, pm, ssk, knit to m, sl m, knit to end—1 st dec'd.

Row 2 and all WS rows: Knit to m, sl m, purl to m, sl m, k2, sl m, p5.

Row 3: K5, sl m, k2, sl m, ssk, knit to m, sl m, k2tog, knit to end—2 sts dec'd.

Rows 5–18: Work Rows 1–4 twice more then Rows 1–2 once more—11 sts rem.

Row 19: (RS) K5, sl m, k2, remove m, ssk, remove m, k2tog—9 sts rem.

Row 20: P2, k2, sl m, p5.

BO and set up fringe: (RS) K5, remove m, BO 4 rem sts. Drop 5 rem sts from needle and let them ravel down to CO edge.

finishing

Finish fringe as directed on page 112. Weave in all ends. Block piece to finished measurements.

LACE EDGING

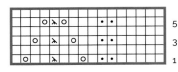

16 sts

	knit on RS; purl on WS
	purl on RS; knit on WS
	yo
	sk2p
	pattern repeat

creating a self-fringing knitted edge

Making fringe can be tedious. Cutting and attaching individual pieces of yarn to a project can take forever. An easy solution is to take advantage of knitted fabric's natural ability to unravel, and knit the fringe as you go! By leaving a margin of plain fabric on the edge of a knitted shape, you can create attached fringe of any length. The loose stitches will unravel lengthwise, but won't unravel widthwise.

This method works especially well for shawls that are worked side to side, such as Rhoeas (shown at right), because the selvedge edge becomes the bottom edge when the shawl is worn. You could also work self-fringe as part of a knitted-on edging.

Begin by determining how many stitches you need to work to create the fringe length you want. Once the stitches are unraveled, how long is the strand of yarn that remains **(figure 1)**? A good rule of thumb is to knit a margin about one-third of the final fringe length, but this can vary with yarn thickness and individual knitter's gauge, so be sure to swatch. Once you determine how many stitches you need to achieve your desired fringe length, add this number to your cast-on number and work the extra stitches in plain stockinette at the outer edge of the project.

Once you've finished knitting your project, bind off all EXCEPT the fringe stitches. Slip your needle out of the fringe stitches. *Use your fingers or a knitting needle to tease apart the first two rows of stitches, resulting in a loose loop of yarn. Tie this loop off with an overhand knot, close to the fabric edge **(figure 2)**. Repeat from * for every fringe loop, ending with your cast-on edge loop.

The resulting fringe will be crinkled and kinked, so you'll need to give it a good steaming. Your secret weapon? A fork! Use a metal fork to keep the fringe loops under slight tension as you hover your iron over the loops, letting them straighten out under the steam. You can then leave your fringe looped or trim each loop to create traditional fringe **(figure 3)**.

Figure 1

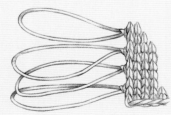

Figure 2

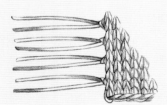

Figure 3

Emmylou
SHAWL

DESIGNED BY **Mercedes Tarasovich**

Short-rows and a gorgeous autumnal-colored yarn create a gently curved wrap that will brighten up your wardrobe. The simple cable patterns are a great way to practice cabling without a cable needle, and the texture of the body and simple lace edging let the gorgeous color and sheen of the yarn sing!

finished size
About 54" (137 cm) wide and 15" (38 cm) deep at center, after blocking.

yarn
Fingering weight (#1 Super Fine).

SHOWN HERE: Hazel Knits Divine (75% superwash merino wool, 15% cashmere, 10% silk; 400 yd [366 m]/4 oz [115 g]): Braeburn, 1 skein.

needles
Size U.S. 6 (4 mm): 32" (80 cm) circular (cir).

Size U.S. E-4 (3.5 mm) crochet hook.

Adjust needle size if necessary to obtain the correct gauge.

notions
Cable needle (cn); tapestry needle.

gauge
18 sts and 24 rows = 4" (10 cm) in Body Chart after blocking.

shawl body

CO 76 sts loosely over both needle tips. Carefully remove second needle tip.

Inc row: (RS) Sl 1, k1, *(k1, yo, k1) in next st; rep from * to last 2 sts, k1, k1 tbl—220 sts.

Set-up row: (WS) Sl 1, k112, turn.

SHORT-ROW SHAPING

Work Body Chart as foll:

Row 1: (RS) Yo, work 6 sts of chart, turn.

Row 2: (WS) Yo, work 9 sts of chart, turn.

Row 3: Yo, work 12 sts of chart, turn.

Row 4: Yo, work 15 sts of chart, working 6-st rep twice, turn.

Continue to work chart in this way, working 3 more sts in each row and working a yarnover at the beg of each row, until Rows 1–12 of Body Chart have been worked 5 times, then work Rows 1–10 once more. Work yarnovers tog in patt with following st on following row using a k2tog or a p2tog.

Row 11: (RS) Yo, work chart row to last 3 sts, k1, p1, k1 tbl.

Row 12: (WS) Work chart row to last st, k1 tbl—220 sts.

LACE EDGING

Work Rows 1–32 of the Edging Chart—404 sts.

CROCHET BIND-OFF

With crochet hook, BO as follows: [insert hook in group of 2 sts, yarn over and draw lp through all sts on hook, ch 6] twice, *insert hook in group of 3 sts, yarn over and draw loop through all sts on hook, ch 6; rep from * to last 4 sts, insert hook in group of 2 sts, yarn over and draw lp through all sts on hook, ch 6, insert hook in group of 2 sts, yarn over and draw through all sts on hook. Fasten off.

finishing

Weave in all ends, but do not trim. Block using desired method into crescent shape, pulling out points on crochet loops. Trim ends.

BODY CHART

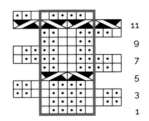

	k on RS; p on WS
	p on RS; k on WS
	k1tbl on RS; p1tbl on WS
	yo
	k2tog
	ssk
	k3tog
	sl 1 wyb on RS; sl 1 wyf on WS
	no stitch
	pattern repeat
	sl 1, k2, pass slipped st over both sts
	sl 2 sts onto cn, hold in back, k1, k2 from cn
	sl 1 st onto cn, hold in front, k2, k1 from cn
	sl 2 sts onto cn, hold in back, k1, p2 from cn
	sl 1 st onto cn, hold in front, p2, k1 from cn

EDGING CHART

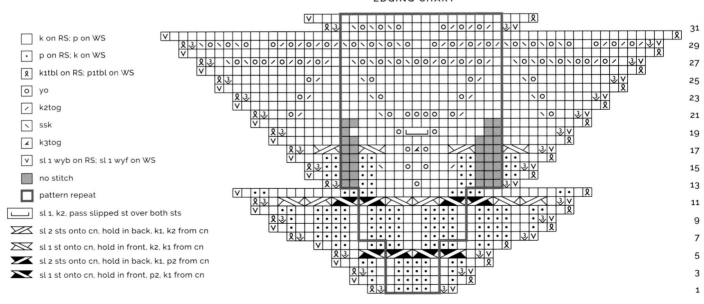

abbreviations

beg	begin(ning)	**LH**	left hand	**ssk**	slip 2 stitches knit-wise one at a time; insert point of left needle into front of 2 slipped stitches and knit them together through back loops with right needle
BO	bind off	**m**	marker(s)		
ch	chain	**M1**	make one (increase)		
cir	circular	**M1P**	make one purl		
cn	cable needle	**p**	purl		
CO	cast on	**p1f&b**	purl into front and back of same stitch		
cont	continue(s); continuing	**p2tog**	purl 2 stitches together	**sssk**	slip 3 stitches knit-wise one at a time; insert point of left needle into front of 3 slipped stitches and knit them together with right needle
dec(s)('d)	decrease(s); decreasing; decreased	**patt(s)**	pattern(s)		
		pm	place marker		
dpn(s)	double-pointed needle(s)	**pwise**	purlwise, as if to purl		
foll(s)	follow(s); following	**rem**	remain(s); remaining	**St st**	stockinette stitch
inc(s)('d)	increase(s); increasing; increased	**rep**	repeat(s); repeating	**st(s)**	stitch(es)
		RH	right hand	**tbl**	through back loop
k	knit	**rnd(s)**	round(s)	**tog**	together
k1f&b	knit into the front and back of the same stitch	**RS**	right side	**WS**	wrong side
		sc	single crochet	**wyb**	with yarn in back
k2tog	knit 2 stitches together	**sl**	slip	**wyf**	with yarn in front
		sl st	slip stitch (crochet)	**yo**	yarnover
k3tog	knit 3 stitches together	**sl1yo**	slip one, yarnover		
kwise	knitwise, as if to knit	**sm**	slip marker		

bind-offs
DECREASE BIND-OFF
Version A

Knitting through the back loops

This version gives a bind-off edge that looks just like a standard bind-off, but it is much stretchier.

Step 1: Knit together the first two stitches on the left needle through the back loop (Figure 1).

Step 2: Slip the new stitch on the right needle back to the left needle (Figure 2).

Step 3: Repeat 1 and 2 until all stitches are bound off.

Notice how the bind-off edge is nearly indistiguishable from your normal bind-off, but give it a tug and you'll see how much more flexible it is.

Version B

Knitting through the front loops

Step 1: Knit together the first two stitches on the left needle (Figure 3).

Step 2: Slip the new stitch on the right needle back to the left needle.

Step 3: Repeat these two steps until all stitches are bound off.

Here, contrasting color yarn is used in the bind-off row so you can see the finished effect more clearly.

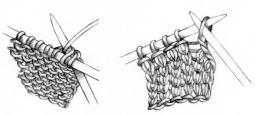

Figure 1   Figure 2

Figure 3   Figure 4

I-CORD BIND-OFF

With right side facing and using the knitted method, cast on three stitches (for cord) onto the end of the needle holding the stitches to be bound off (Figure 1) , *k2, k2tog through back loops (the last cord stitch with the first stitch to be bound off; (Figure 2) , slip these three stitches back to the left needle (Figure 3) , and pull the yarn firmly from the back. Repeat from * until three stitches remain on left needle and no stitches remain on right needle. Bind off remaining stitches using the standard method.

K2TOG BIND-OFF

This bind-off gives a very elastic edge without needing to change needle size or tension.
K2, *slip both sts back to left needle, k2togtbl, k1, rep from * until all sts are BO.

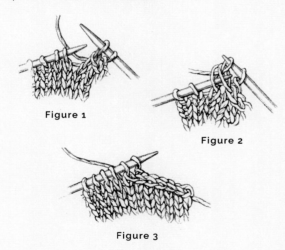

Figure 1

Figure 2

Figure 3

GATHERED CROCHET BIND-OFF

Insert hook through the back legs of the specified number of stitches (Figure 1; three stitches shown) to gather them, pull a loop through so there is one loop on the hook (Figure 2), work a crochet chain the specified length (Figure 3; eight stitches shown), *insert the crochet hook through the back legs of the next group of stitches (Figure 4), pull the yarn loop through these stitches as well as through the stitch of the chain (Figure 5), and work a crochet chain for the specified number of stitches; repeat from *.

If working in rounds, finish by joining the final chain to the base of the first gathered group, then pull the yarn through the final loop, leaving a 9" (23 cm) tail.

If working in rows, finish by pulling the loop through the final group of stitches, then pulling the yarn through the final loop, leaving a 9" (23 cm) tail.

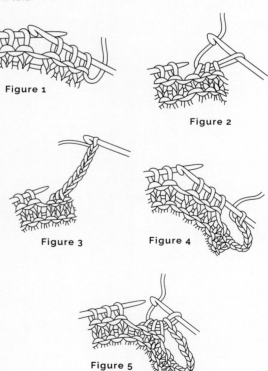

Figure 1

Figure 2

Figure 3

Figure 4

Figure 5

cast-ons

BACKWARD-LOOP CAST-ON

*Loop working yarn and place it on needle backward so that it doesn't unwind. Repeat from *.

CABLE CAST-ON

If there are no established stitches, begin with a slipknot, knit one stitch in slipknot and slip this new stitch to left needle. *Insert right needle between first two stitches on left needle (Figure 1). Wrap yarn as if to knit. Draw yarn through to complete stitch (Figure 2) and slip this new stitch to left needle as shown (Figure 3). Repeat from *

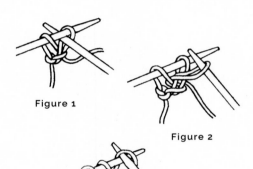

Figure 1

Figure 2

Figure 3

KNITTED CAST-ON

Place slipknot on left needle if there are no established stitches. *With right needle, knit into first stitch (or slipknot) on left needle (Figure 1) and place new stitch onto left needle (Figure 2). Repeat from *, always knitting into last stitch made.

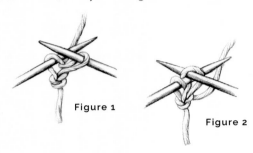

Figure 1

Figure 2

PROVISIONAL CAST-ON

Place a loose slipknot on needle held in your right hand. Hold waste yarn next to slipknot and around left thumb; hold working yarn over left index finger. *Bring needle forward under waste yarn, over working yarn, grab a loop of working yarn (Figure 1), then bring needle to the front, over both yarns, and grab a second loop (Figure 2). Repeat from *. When you're ready to use the cast-on stitches, pick out waste yarn to expose live stitches.

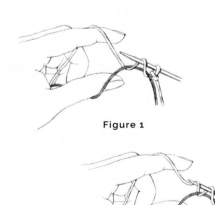

Figure 1

Figure 2

decreases

KNIT 2 TOGETHER (K2TOG)

Knit two stitches together as if they were a single stitch.

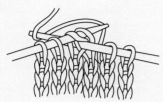

KNIT 3 TOGETHER (K3TOG)

Knit three stitches together as if they were a single stitch.

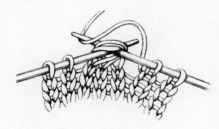

SLIP, SLIP, KNIT (SSK)

Slip two stitches individually knitwise (Figure 1), insert left needle tip into the front of these two slipped stitches, and use the right needle to knit them together through their back loops (Figure 2).

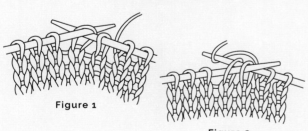

Figure 1

Figure 2

duplicate stitch

DUPLICATE STITCH ON STOCKINETTE STITCH

Horizontal

Bring threaded needle out from back to front at the base of the V of the knitted stitch you want to cover. *Working right to left, pass needle in and out under the stitch in the row above it and back into the base of the same stitch. Bring needle back out at the base of the V of the next stitch to the left. Repeat from *.

Vertical

Beginning at lowest point, work as for horizontal duplicate stitch, ending by bringing the needle back out at the base of the stitch directly above the stitch just worked.

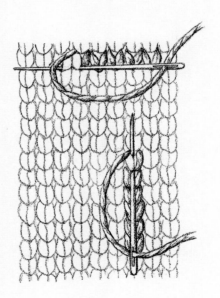

DUPLICATE STITCH ON REVERSE STOCKINETTE STITCH

Thread yarn to be woven in on tapestry needle. Working from right to left, insert tapestry needle up into a purl bump. *Following the path of the underlying stitch, insert needle into the next purl bump to the upper right of first bump (Figure 1). Continue following the path of the yarn and, bringing needle down, insert needle down into next purl bump to the left, then back down through the first purl bump (Figure 2). Follow the path of the yarn and insert needle up through the next purl bump to the left, then repeat from *.

DUPLICATE STITCH ON GARTER STITCH

Thread yarn to be woven in on tapestry needle. Working from right to left, insert needle up through a purl bump (Figure 1) . *Following the path of the underlying stitch, bring needle down through next purl bump to the left (Figure 2) . Spread garter-stitch fabric out and find the stockinette row below the purl bump you're working on. Insert needle from right to left under the legs of the knit stitch below last purl bump entered (Figure 3) . Bring needle up and insert needle back up through last purl bump entered. Repeat from *.

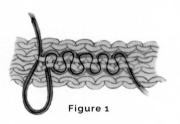

Figure 1

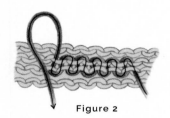

Figure 2

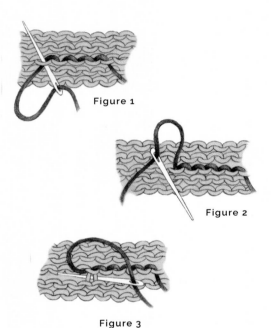

Figure 1

Figure 2

Figure 3

increases

BAR INCREASE

Knitwise (k1f&b)

Knit into a stitch but leave the stitch on the left needle (Figure 1), then knit through the back loop of the same stitch (Figure 2) and slip the original stitch off the needle (Figure 3).

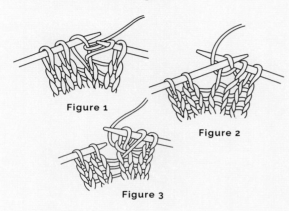

Figure 1

Figure 2

Figure 3

Purlwise (p1f&b)

Work as for a knitwise bar increase, but purl into the front and back of the same stitch.

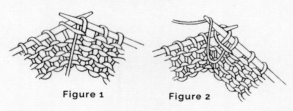

Figure 1

Figure 2

LIFTED INCREASE (LI)

Right Slant (RLI)

Knit into the back of the stitch (in the "purl bump") in the row directly below the "first stitch on the left needle (Figure 1), then knit the stitch on the needle (Figure 2) and slip the original stitch off the needle.

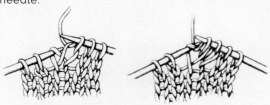

Figure 1

Figure 2

Left Slant (LLI)

Insert left needle from front to back into the stitch below stitch just knitted (Figure 3). Knit this stitch (Figure 4).

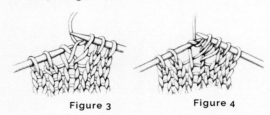

Figure 3

Figure 4

MAKE 1 (M1) INCREASES

Left Slant (M1L) and Standard M1

With left needle tip, lift strand between needles from front to back (Figure 1). Knit lifted loop through the back (Figure 2).

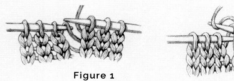

Figure 1

Figure 2

Right Slant (M1R)

With left needle tip, lift strand between needles from back to front (Figure 1). Knit lifted loop through the front (Figure 2)

Purl (M1P)

For purl versions, work as above, purling lifted loop.

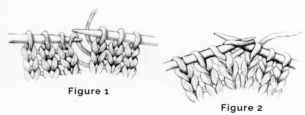

Figure 1

Figure 2

pick up and knit

ALONG CAST-ON OR BIND-OFF EDGE

With right side facing and working from right to left, insert the tip of the needle into the center of the stitch below the bind-off or cast-on edge (Figure 1), wrap yarn around needle, and pull through a loop (Figure 2). Pick up one stitch for every existing stitch.

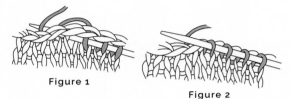

Figure 1

Figure 2

ALONG SHAPED EDGE

With right side facing and working from right to left, insert tip of needle between last and second-to-last stitches, wrap yarn around needle, and pull through a loop. Pick up and knit about three stitches for every four rows, adjusting as necessary so that picked-up edge lays flat.

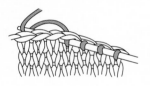

pick up and purl

With wrong side of work facing and working from right to left, *insert needle tip under purl stitch in the last row from the far side to the near side (Figure 1), wrap yarn around needle, and pull a loop through (Figure 2). Repeat from * for desired number of stitches.

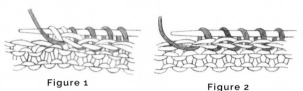

Figure 1

Figure 2

short-row

Work to turn point, slip next stitch purlwise to right needle. Bring yarn to front (Figure 1). Slip same stitch back to left needle (Figure 2). Turn work and bring yarn in position for next stitch, wrapping the slipped stitch as you do so.

Note: Hide wraps on a knit stitch when right side of piece is worked as a knit stitch. Leave wrap if the purl stitch shows on the right side. Hide wraps as follows:

Knit Stitch: On right side, work to just before wrapped stitch, insert right needle from front, under the wrap from bottom up, and then into wrapped stitch as usual. Knit them together, making sure the new stitch comes out under wrap.

Purl Stitch: On wrong side, work to just before wrapped stitch. Insert right needle from back, under wrap from bottom up, and put on left needle. Purl lifted wrap and stitch together.

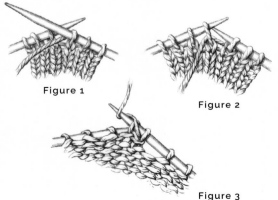

Figure 1

Figure 2

Figure 3

about the designers

Andrea Jurgrau is a nurse practitioner and avid lace knitter. Her patterns have appeared in *KnitScene*, *Vogue Knitting*, *Spin·Off*, and more. Her first book, *New Heights in Lace Knitting*, was published in 2016. She resides in New York.
website: badcatdesigns.blogspot.com

Carol Feller enjoys designing knitwear that is flattering to wear and enjoyable to knit. She is the author of several books including *Short Row Knits* (Potter Craft, 2015), and *Contemporary Irish Knits* (Wiley, 2011). Carol lives in the south of Ireland.
website: stolenstitches.com

Corrina Ferguson is the designer behind Picnic Knits. An active designer, editor, and teacher, Corrina has over 200 patterns to her credit. She is the author of *Warm Days, Cool Knits* (Interweave, 2015).
website: corrinaferguson.com

Courtney Kelley is the co-owner of Kelbourne Woolens, distributors of The Fibre Company yarns. Her designs have appeared in *25 Knitted Accessories*, *Fair Isle Style*, *Weekend Hats*, and more. She is the coauthor of *November Knits* (Interweave, 2012) and *Vintage Modern Knits* (Interweave, 2011).
website: kelbournewoolens.com

Joan Forgione is a mother, knitwear designer, and teacher. Her designs have been published in *Vogue Knitting*, *Interweave Knits*, *KNIT (UK)*, *Knit Now*, *Knit Simple*, and more.
website: papermoonknits.com

Kristin Omdahl designs knit and crochet garments and patterns and sells her own line of yarn and more. She also designs for several knitting and crochet magazines such as *Interweave Crochet*, *Crochet Today,* and *Crochet!* She is the author of several books including *Continuous Crochet* (Interweave, 2016) and *Crochet So Lovely* (Interweave, 2015).
website: kristinomdahl.com

Lee Meredith is a maker of things, doer of stuff living in Portland, Oregon. She focuses on patterns that are fun to make, teach new concepts, and feature different style options and variations.
website: lethalknits.com

Lisa Shroyer, former editor of *Knitscene* and *Interweave Knits* magazines, is now the Content Strategist for Yarn and Fiber at Interweave. She is the author of *Knitting Plus* (Interweave, 2011) and *The Best of Knitscene* (2011).

Lucinda Guy is a knitwear designer-maker, tutor, and author of ten knitting, crochet, and stitch books, including *First Frost* (Interweave, 2014) and *Northern Knits Gifts* (Interweave, 2012). She lives in Brighton on the south England coast.
website: lucindaguy.com

Manda Shah designs for both knit and crochet. Her patterns primarily feature lacework. Manda's patterns have appeared in *Knitting Traditions*, *Interweave Knits*, *I Like Knitting*, *Twist Collective*, and more. Find her on Ravelry under username "MSCin."

Megi Burcl is a knitwear designer who favors irreverent color combinations and garter stitch. Her designs are often featured in *Knitscene* magazine and other publications. Find her on Ravelry under the username "megi."

Melissa Wehrle works for a knitwear company on Seventh Avenue. In her spare time, she designs patterns that have been featured in *Knitscene, Twist Collective*, *Interweave Knits*, and several books. Her first book, *Metropolitan Knits* was published by *Interweave* in 2013. Melissa lives in Astoria, New York, with her husband.
website: neoknits.com

Mercedes Tarasovich, a former yarn shop owner and dyer, now focuses full-time on knitwear design. Her designs can be seen in *Interweave Knits*, *Knitscene*, *Twist Collective*, *Knitty*, and more. Her first book, *Brioche Chic*, was published in 2014.
website: mercedesknits.com

Nancy Bush has been working in the world of knitting for over thirty years. Her books reflect her passion for Estonian knitting and include such classics as *Folk Knitting in Estonia* (Interweave, 2000) and *Knitted Lace of Estonia* (Interweave, 2010).
website: woolywest.com

Susanna IC is an artist by calling and an art historian by training who strives to make lace knitting fun and manageable for even novice knitters. Her designs have appeared in numerous publications including *Interweave Knits*, *Twist Collective*, *Wool People*, and *Knitty*.
website: artqualia.com

Tabetha Hedrick creates designs that are classic, beautiful, and fun to knit. Her designs have been published in numerous books, magazines, and collections including *Creative Knitting*, *Knitscene*, *Tangled*, *Classic Elite*, and more.
website: tabethahedrick.com

sources for yarn

Anzula
740 H St.
Fresno, CA 93721
anzula.com

Berroco Inc.
1 Tupperware Dr., Ste. 4
N. Smithfield, RI 02896
berroco.com

Blue Sky Alpacas
PO Box 88
Cedar, MN 55011
blueskyalpacas.com

Cascade Yarns
PO Box 58168
1224 Andover Park E.
Tukwila, WA 98188
cascadeyarns.com

Dream in Color
907 Atlantic Ave.
West Chicago, IL 60185
dreamincoloryarn.com
Elemental Affects
17555 Bubbling Wells Rd.
Desert Hot Springs, CA
92241
elementalaffects.com

Hazel Knits
PO Box 28921
Seattle, WA 98118
hazelknits.com

Jade Sapphire
jadesapphire.com
Kelbourne Woolens
915 North 28th St,
second floor
Philadelphia, PA 19130
kelbournewoolens.com

Lara's Creations
909 Pinon Ct.
Longmont, CO 80504
etsy.com/shop/larascreations

Loðband
Ístex
PO Box 140
270 Mosfellsbær
Iceland
www.istex.is

Madelinetosh Co.
3436 Alemeda St., Ste. #229
Fort Worth, TX, 76126
madelinetosh.com

Plymouth Yarn Company Inc.
500 Lafayette Street
Bristol, PA 19007
plymouthyarn.com

Sundara Yarn
PO Box 1118
Carlsborg, WA 98324
sundarayarn.com

Shibui Knits
shibuiknits.com
Vijay Fibers
vijayfibers.com

METRIC CONVERSION

TO CONVERT	TO	MULTIPLY BY
Inches	Centimeters	2.54
Centimeters	Inches	0.4
Feet	Centimeters	30.5
Centimeters	Feet	0.03
Yards	Meters	0.9
Meters	Yards	1.1

www.fwcommunity.com

21 20 19 18 17   5 4 3 2 1

Distributed in Canada by Fraser Direct
100 Armstrong Avenue
Georgetown, ON, Canada L7G 5S4
Tel: (905) 877-4411

Distributed in the U.K. and Europe
by F&W MEDIA INTERNATIONAL
F&W Media International Ltd.
Pynes Hill Court
Pynes Hill
Rydon Lane
Exeter
EX2 5SP
United Kingdom
Tel: (+44) 1626-323236
E-mail: enquiries@fwmedia.com

SRN: 17KN05
ISBN-13: 978-1-63250-600-9

Curated and Edited by Stephanie White
Cover Design by Elisabeth Laviere
Interior Design by Karla Baker
Photography by Joe Hancock
Production coordinated by Bryan Davidson

find more classic patterns in these great books!

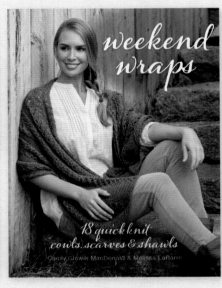

The Knitted Hat Book
20 Knitted Beanies, Tams, Cloches, and More

Interweave Editors
978-1-63250-221-6
$22.99

Weekend Wraps
18 Quick Knit Cowls, Scarves & Shawls

Cecily Glowik MacDonald & Melissa LaBarre
978-1-63250-278-0
$24.99

Garter Stitch Revival
20 Creative Knitting Patterns Featuring the Simplest Stitch

Interweave Editors
978-1-63250-298-8
$24.99

Available at your favorite retailer, or Interweave.com